COGAT®
GRADE 3
NON-VERBAL

3 Practice Tests
Level 9

Savant Test Prep™

www.SavantPrep.com

Please leave a review for this book!

Thank you for purchasing this resource.

Please take a moment to leave a
review on the website where you purchased this.

TABLE OF CONTENTS

INTRODUCTION

PRACTICE TEST 1 (WORKBOOK FORMAT)

PRACTICE TEST 2

PRACTICE TEST 3

ANSWER KEYS

INTRODUCTION

COGAT® GENERAL INFORMATION

- COGAT® stands for Cognitive Abilities Test®.
- The test measures students' reasoning skills and problem-solving skills.
- It provides educators with an overall assessment of students' academic strengths and weaknesses.
- The COGAT® is commonly used as a screener for gifted and talented programs.
    - Gifted and Talented (G&T) selection sometimes requires a teacher recommendation as well.
- The test is usually administered in a group setting.
- A teacher (or other school associate) administers the test, reading the directions.
- Please check with your school/testing site regarding its testing procedures, as these may differ.

COGAT® LEVEL 9 FORMAT

- Students in third grade take the COGAT® Level 9.
- The Non-Verbal Battery has 56 questions.
- The test is divided into 3 main parts, each called a "Battery." Each Battery has three question types. See the chart below.

VERBAL BATTERY	NON-VERBAL BATTERY	QUANTITATIVE BATTERY
Verbal Analogies: 22 Questions	Figure Analogies: 20 Questions	Number Puzzles: 16 Questions
Verbal Classification: 20 Questions	Figure Classification: 20 Questions	Number Series: 18 Questions
Sentence Completion: 20 Questions	Paper Folding: 16 Questions	Number Analogies: 18 Questions

- Often, schools administer one Battery per day, allowing approximately 45 minutes per Battery.
- Students have around 15 minutes to complete each question type (for example, students would have around 15 minutes to complete Verbal Analogies).
- See the following pages for examples and explanations of each question type.

COGAT® SCORING

- Students receive points for correct answers. Points are not deducted for incorrect answers. (Therefore, students should at least guess versus leaving a question blank.)
- In general, schools have a "cut-off" COGAT® score, which they consider together with additional criteria, for gifted & talented acceptance. This varies by school.
- This score is usually at least 98%. (However, some schools accept scores of 95% or even 85%.)
- A score of 98% means that your child scored as well as, or better than, 98% of those in his/her testing group.
- COGAT® scores are available for the entire test and can be broken down by Battery.
- Depending on the school/program, such a "cut-off" score may only be required on one or two of the Batteries (and not on the test overall).
- It is essential to check with your school/program for their acceptance procedures.
- The COGAT® Practice Tests in this book can not yield these percentiles because they have not been given to a large enough group of students to produce an accurate comparison/calculation.

HOW TO USE THIS BOOK

1. Go over the Question Examples together with your child. These begin on the next page.

2. Do Practice Test 1 (Workbook Format)
   - Do these questions with your child, especially if this is your child's first exposure to COGAT®-prep questions. These questions have a "workbook format," meaning they are meant to be done together.
   - Do not assign a time limit.
   - Talk about what the question is asking your child to do.
   - Questions progress in difficulty. (The first few questions are quite simple.)
   - Go over the answers using the Answer Key.
   - For questions missed, go over the answers again, discussing what makes the correct answer better than the other choices.

3. Do the remaining Practice Tests following Practice Test 1.
   - If your child progressed easily through Practice Test 1, see how well they can do without your help.
   - If your child needed assistance with much of Practice Test 1, then continue to assist your child with Practice Test 2.
   - If you wish to assign a time limit, assign around 15 minutes per question type.
   - Go over the answers using the Answer Key.
   - For questions missed, go over the answers again, discussing what makes the correct answer better than the other choices.

4. **Need more practice?**

   - **Get 300+ new questions per book.**

   - **Check out Savant Test Prep™ books on Amazon®.**

TEST-TAKING TIPS

- Ensure your child listens carefully to the directions, especially in the Sentence Completion section.
- Make sure (s)he does not rush through questions. (There is no prize for finishing first!) Tell your child to look carefully at the question. Then, tell your child to look at each answer choice before marking his/her answer.
  - If you notice your child continuing to rush through the questions, tell him/her to point to each part of the question. Then, point to each answer choice.
- If (s)he does not know the answer, then use the process of elimination. Cross out any answer choices which are clearly incorrect, then choose from those remaining.
- This tip/suggestion is entirely at your discretion. You may wish to offer some sort of special motivation to encourage your child to do his/her best. An extra incentive of, for example, an art set, a building block set, or a special outing can go a long way in motivating young learners!
- The night before testing, it is imperative that children have enough sleep, without any interruptions. (Think about the difference in **your** brain function with a good night's sleep vs. without. The same goes for your child's brain function.)
- The morning before the test, ensure your child eats a healthy breakfast with protein and complex carbs. Do not let them eat sugar, chocolate, etc.
- If you can choose the time your child will take the test (for example, if (s)he will take the test individually, instead of at school with a group), opt for a morning testing session, when your child will be most alert.

QUESTION EXAMPLES

- Here is an overview of the COGAT® question types.
- This section has <u>simple</u> examples, to introduce your child to test concepts.
    - Do these examples together with your child.
- Below the questions are explanations for parents.

1. FIGURE ANALOGIES (NON-VERBAL BATTERY)

• **Directions (read to child):** The pictures in the top boxes go together in some way. Look at the bottom boxes. One box is empty. Look at the row of pictures next to the boxes. These are the answer choices. Which one of these choices goes with the picture in the bottom box like the pictures in the top box go together?

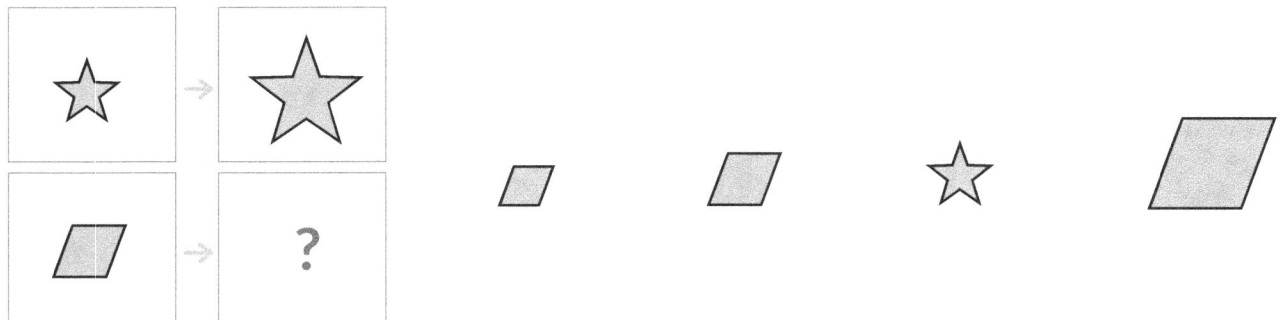

• **Using this question as an example, say to your child:** In the top left box, we see 1 star. In the top right box, we also see a star, but it has gotten bigger. Let's come up with a rule to describe how the picture has changed from left to right. From left to right, the shape gets bigger. On the bottom is a parallelogram. Let's look at the answer choices and see if any fit our rule. The first choice does not - the shape is smaller. The second choice does not - the shape is the same size. The third choice does not - it is a different shape. The last choice does - it is the same shape as the bottom box, but it is bigger.

• **Explanation (for parents):** In the directions, the word "picture" means a "figure" consisting of one or more shapes/lines/etc.

Your child must figure out how the images in the top set of boxes are related and belong together. Then, (s)he must figure out which answer choice would go with the bottom left image so that the bottom set would have the same analogous relationship as the top set. (The small arrows demonstrate that the images go together.)

Try to define a "rule" to describe how the top set belongs together.

Make your "rule" describe a "change" that occurs from the top left box to the top right box.

Next, take this "rule" describing the change, and apply it to the bottom picture.

Then, look at the answer choices to determine which one would make the bottom set also follow your "rule."

If more than one answer choice fits the rule, then the rule needs to be more specific.

- The images below outline "changes" in Figure Analogy questions (how the figures change in the analogy).

- In basic Figure Analogy questions, like the example, there is one "change" -or- a change that is quite obvious.

- In the below images #1-9, there is one change.

- More advanced questions, like #10-12 below, have two changes (or changes that are not as obvious).

Directions for the below images:
- See if your child can figure out how the first picture "changes" to the second picture below.
- The questions' "change" (the logic) is at the bottom of the page.

1.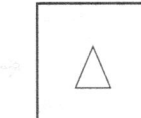

2.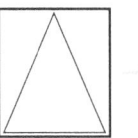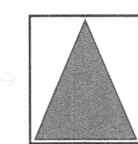

3.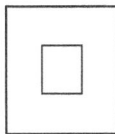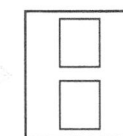

4.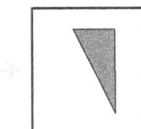

5.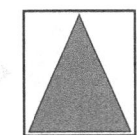

6.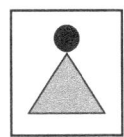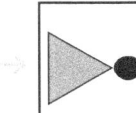

7.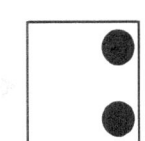

8.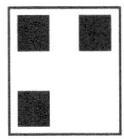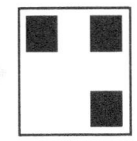

9.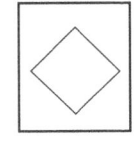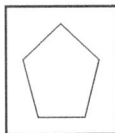

10.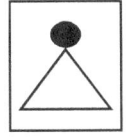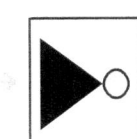

11.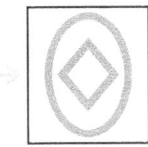

12.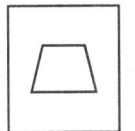

1. Size (gets smaller)
2. Color (white to dark gray)
3. Quantity (plus 1)
4. Whole to Half
5. Color Reversal
6. Rotation (clockwise, 90°)

7. Rotation (clockwise, 90°)
8. Rotation -or- Mirror Image/"Flip"
9. Number of Shape Sides (shape with +1 side)
10. Two Changes: Rotation (clockwise, 90°) and Color Reversal
11. Two Change: Shape Position and Size
12. Two Changes: Shape Size and Color

2. FIGURE CLASSIFICATION (NON-VERBAL BATTERY)

• **Directions (read to child):** The top row shows three pictures that are alike in some way. Look at the bottom row. There are four pictures. Which picture in the bottom row goes best with the pictures in the top row?

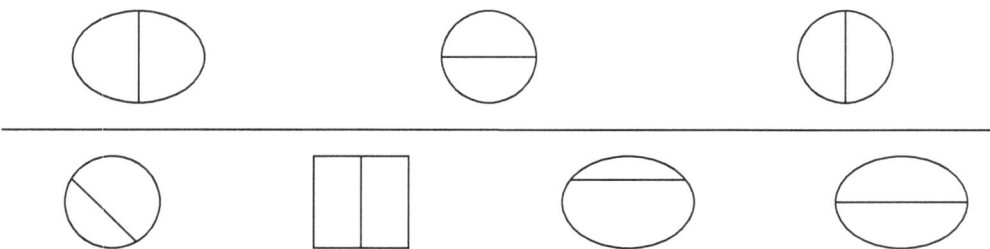

• **Explanation (for parents):** Together with your child, try to figure out a "rule" describing how the top pictures are alike and belong together. Then, apply the "rule" to each answer choice to determine which one follows it. If your child finds that more than one choice follows the rule, then a more specific rule is needed.

• **Using the above question as an example, say to your child:** Here we see 1 oval divided in half, 1 circle divided in half, and 1 circle divided in half. What is a rule that describes how they are alike? They are all round and divided in half. In the bottom row, which choice follows this rule? Choice 1 and 3 are round and divided, but they are not divided in half. Choice 2 is divided in half but not round. Choice 4 is round and divided in half.

• The following examples include basic logic used in Figure Classification questions, with answers at the end.

• **Directions (read to child):** The top row shows three pictures that are alike in some way. Look at the bottom row. There are four pictures. Which picture in the bottom row goes best with the pictures in the top row?

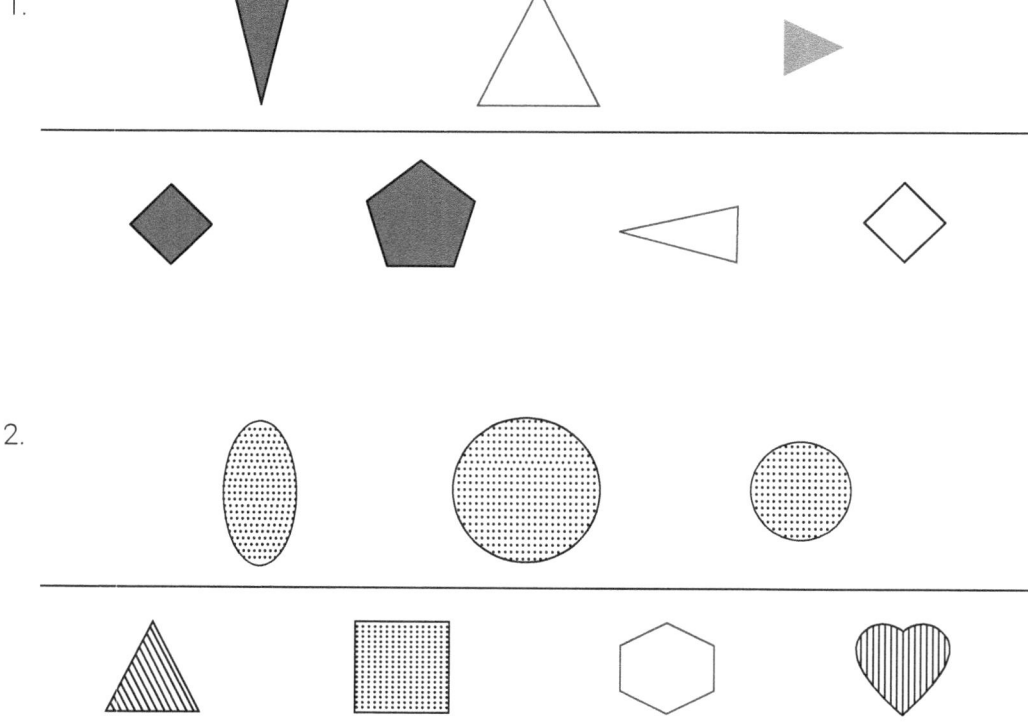

• **Note:** These are <u>more challenging</u>. If your child needs help, ask them the question next to the number.

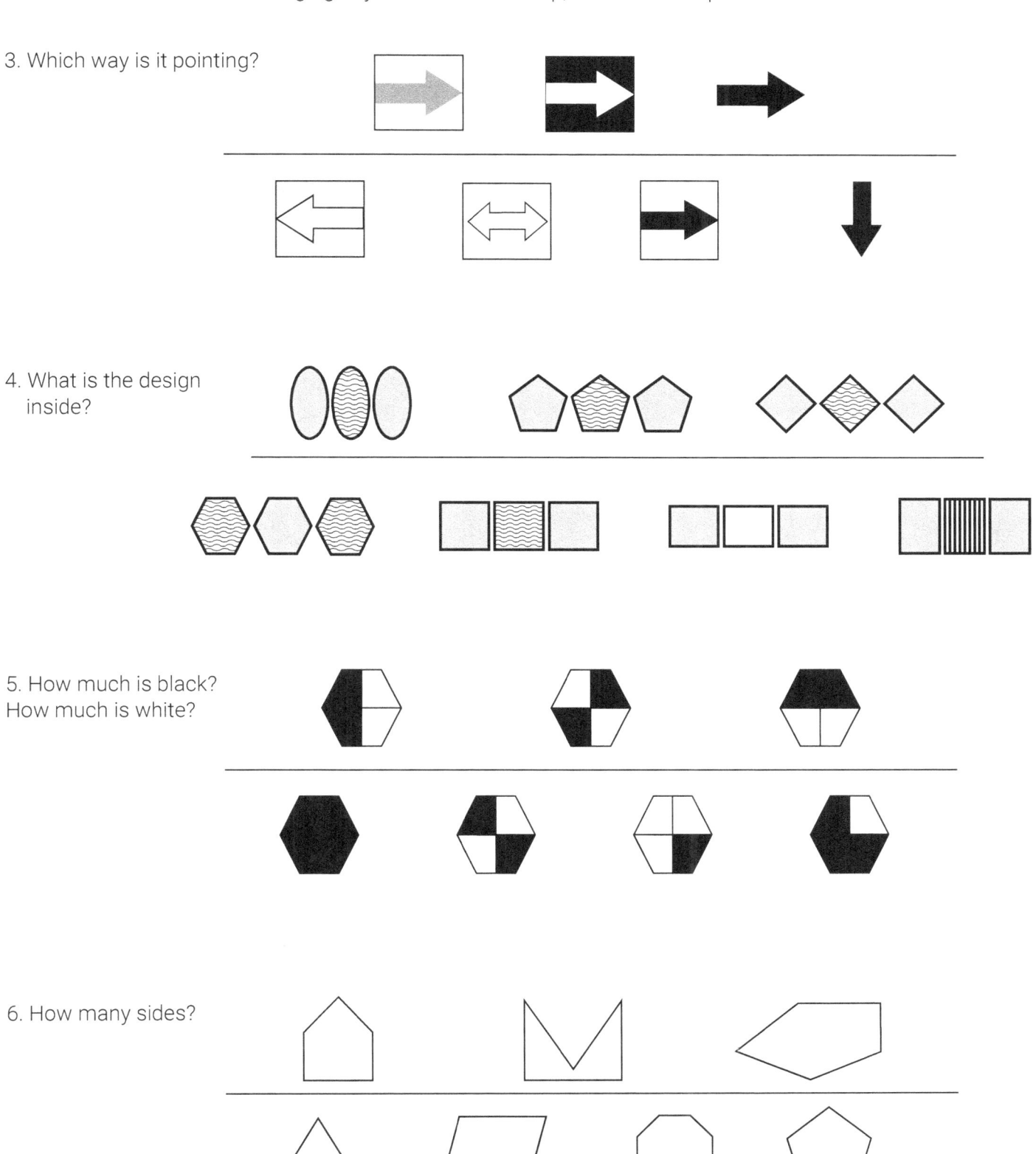

3. Which way is it pointing?

4. What is the design inside?

5. How much is black? How much is white?

6. How many sides?

1-Choice 3: triangles   2-Choice 2: filled with dots   3-Choice 3: arrows point right
4-Choice 2: the designs are gray, wavy lines, gray   5-Choice 2: half is white, half is black
6-Choice 4: the shapes have 5 sides

7. How many shapes of each kind are together next to each other?

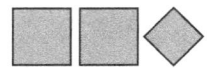  

8. What kind of small shapes are there?

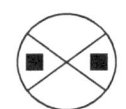  

9. What kinds of shape are gray or white? How many?

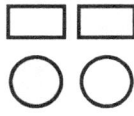  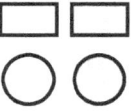

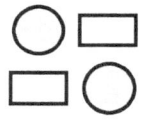  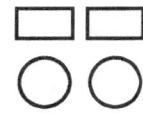 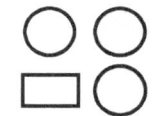

10. How many shapes are in each group?

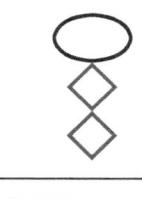 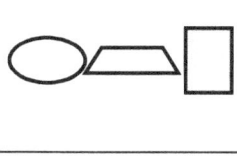 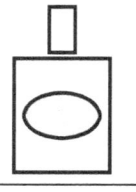

 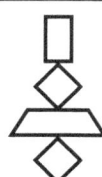 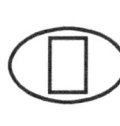 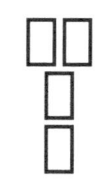

7-Choice 3: there are 2 identical shapes next to a shape that's a different kind of shape
8-Choice 4: the 2 small black shapes are the same
9-Choice 3: the 2 gray shapes are 1 rectangle and 1 circle   10-Choice 1: there are 3 shapes in the group

10

3. PAPER FOLDING (NON-VERBAL BATTERY)

• **Directions (read to child):** The top row of pictures shows a sheet of paper. The paper was folded, then something was cut out. Which picture in the bottom row shows how the paper would look after its unfolded?

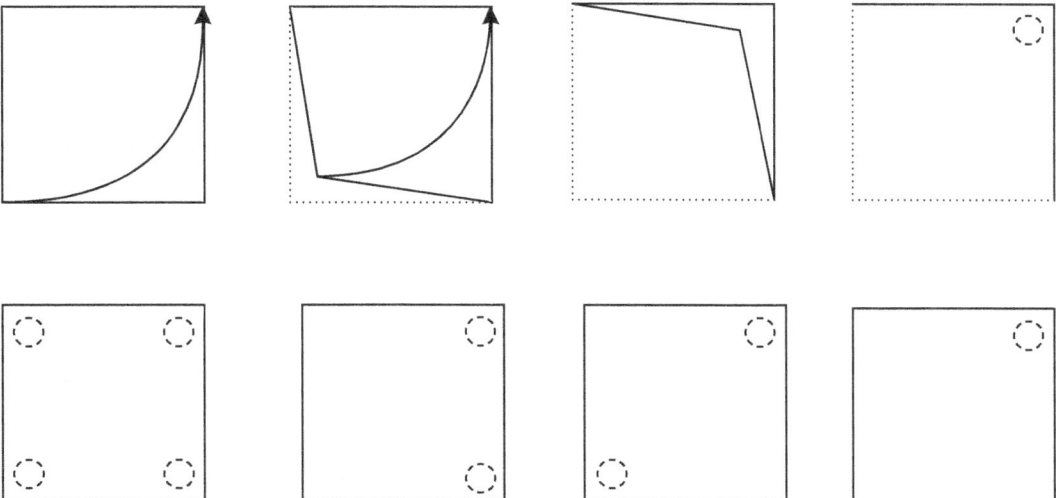

• **Explanation (read to child):** The first choice has too many holes. In the second choice, the holes are not in the correct position. The third choice has the correct number of holes and in the correct position. The last choice only shows the hole on top.

• **Tip:** If Paper Folding is challenging for your child, demonstrate using real paper and scissors. (It is common for kids to initially struggle with Paper Folding. It is not an activity most children have much experience with.)

• Show your child the following examples. Demonstrate using real paper, if needed.

Paper Folding Steps   Result

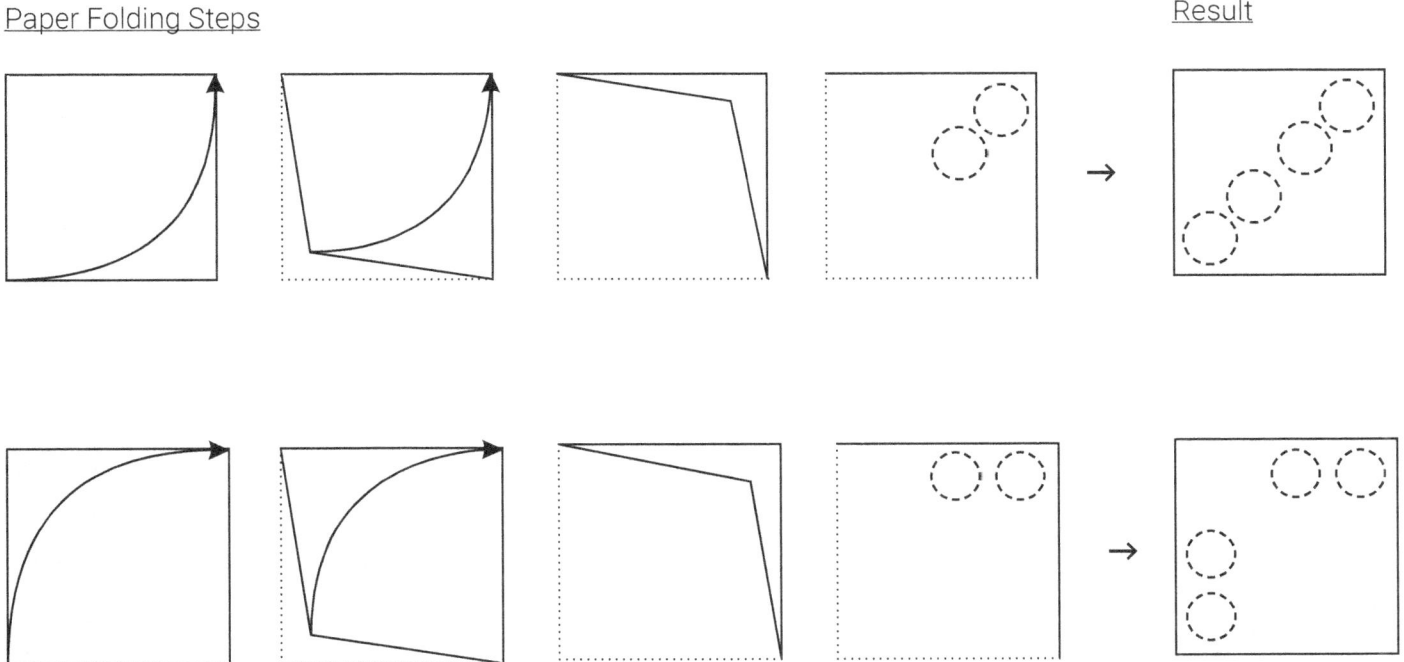

(In the question at the top of the page, the third choice is correct.)

In the example, point out to your child that when the paper is unfolded the triangles point toward each other.

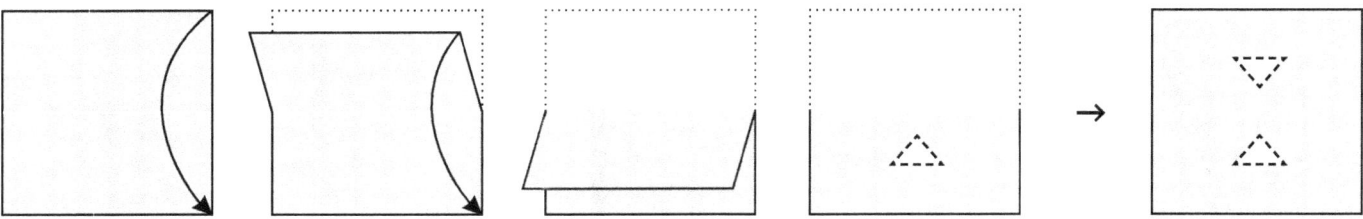

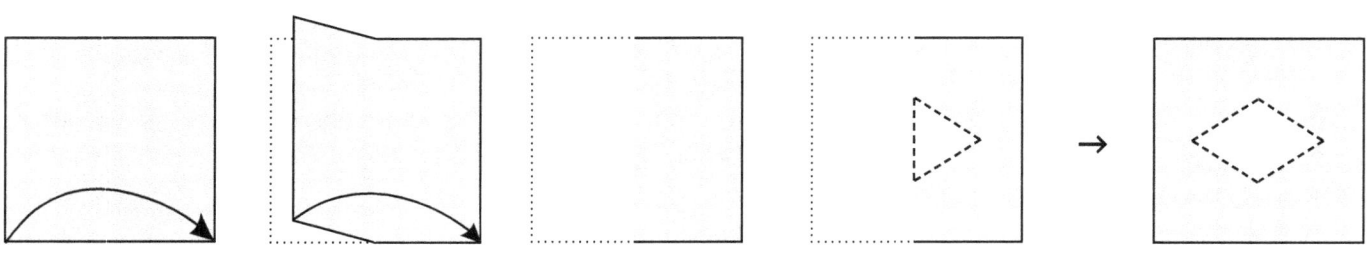

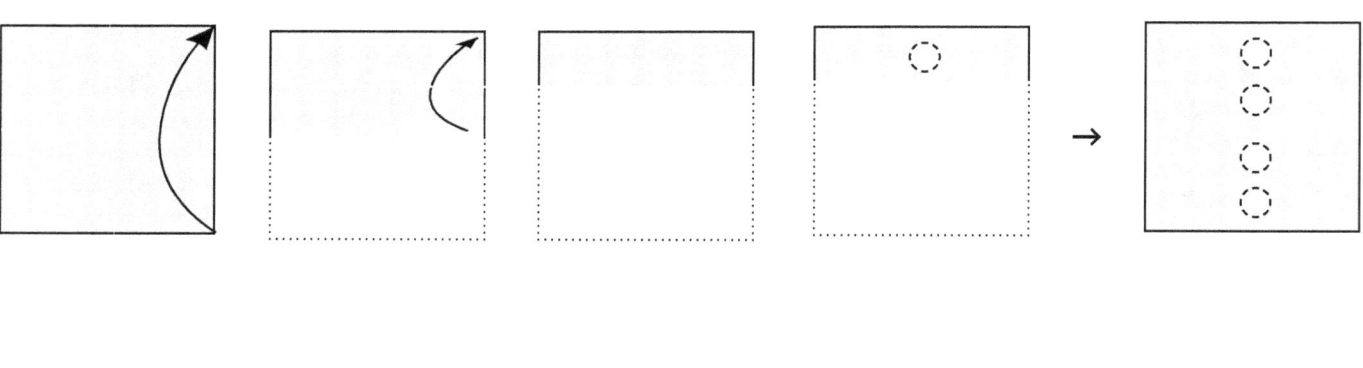

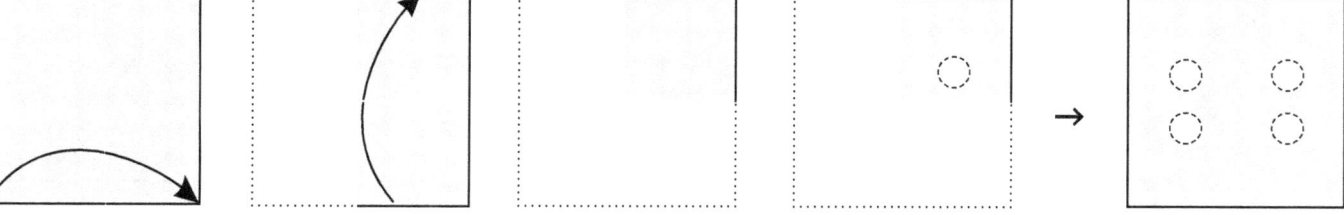

Parents, read the below with your child.

Watch out!

This book is filled with tricky questions. Can you answer them?

Of course you can!

Pay close attention to each question and try your best.

We'll be here to help you along the way!

Practice Test 1 (Workbook Format) begins on the next page.

FIGURE ANALOGIES

Sara

What goes in the box?

Directions: The pictures in the top boxes go together in some way. Look at the bottom boxes. One box is empty. Look at the row of pictures next to the boxes. These are the answer choices. Which one of these choices goes with the picture in the bottom box like the pictures in the top boxes go together?

Explanation (for parents): A more detailed explanation and a Figure Analogies example question is on p.6. If you have not already, look over p.6. Try to define a "rule" to describe how the top set belongs together. With Figure Analogies, this "rule" could describe a "change" that occurs from the top left box to the top right box. Next, take this "rule" describing the change, and apply it to the bottom picture.

Example: First, we see a larger gray circle with a smaller white circle inside. Next, we see this same shape group, but a small gray circle has been added to the middle. Our rule is that the shape group changes and a smaller gray version of that same kind of shape is in the middle.

Let's look in the bottom box. We see another gray and white shape group. This time there are rectangles. Which answer choice follows our rule? Find the choice that shows the same shape group as we first saw, but has a smaller gray version in the middle. Choice A is the right answer.

1

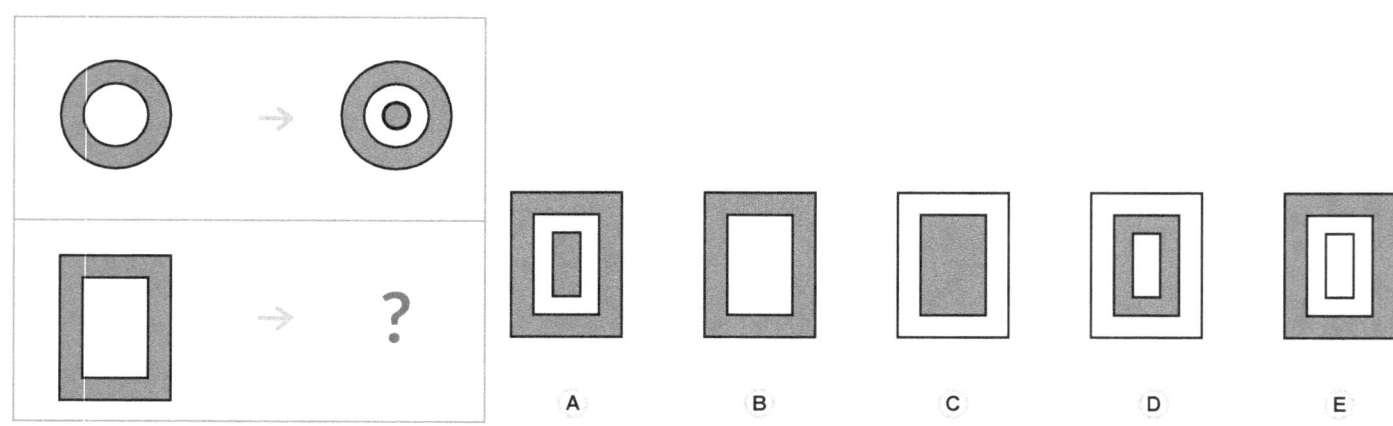

2

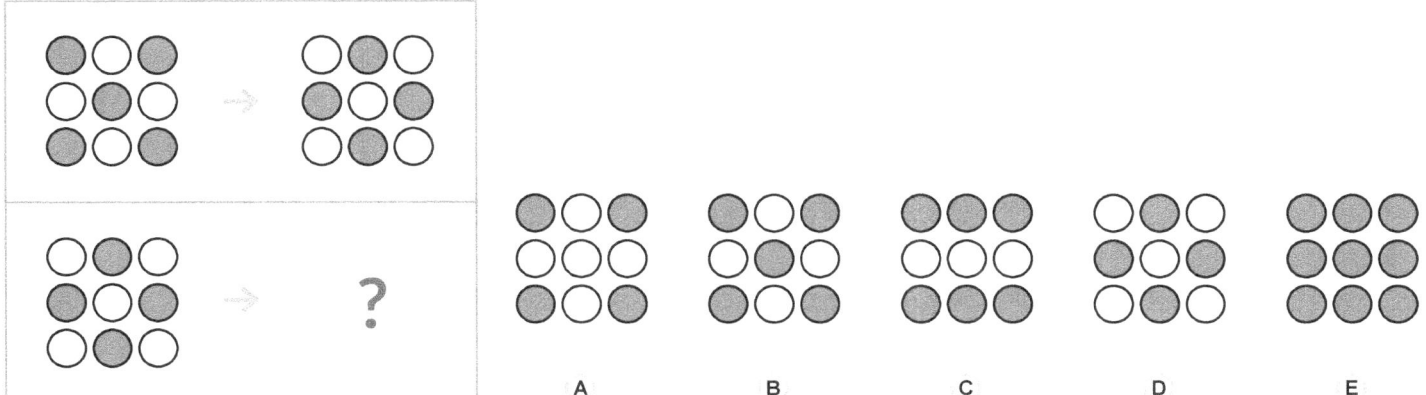

A   B   C   D   E

3

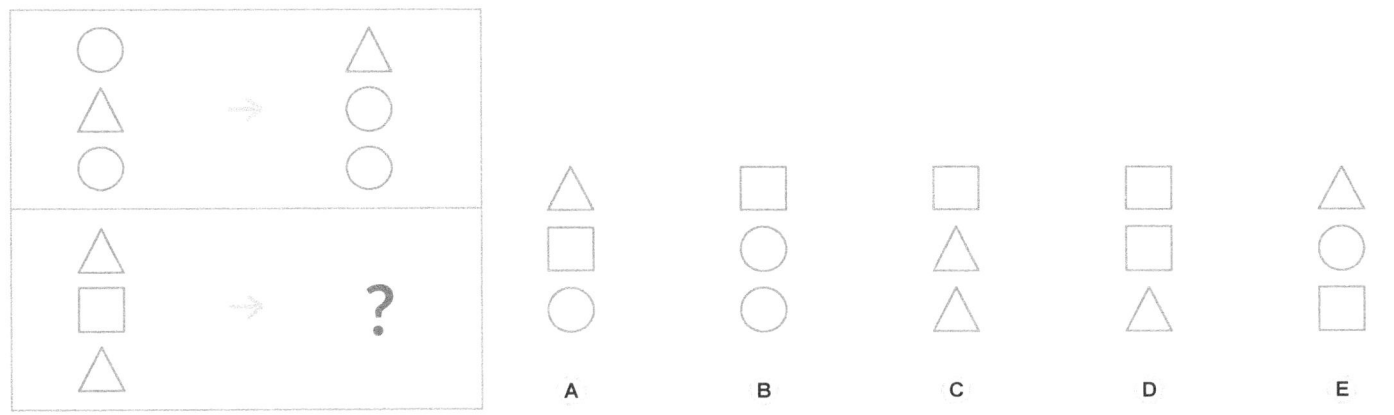

A   B   C   D   E

4

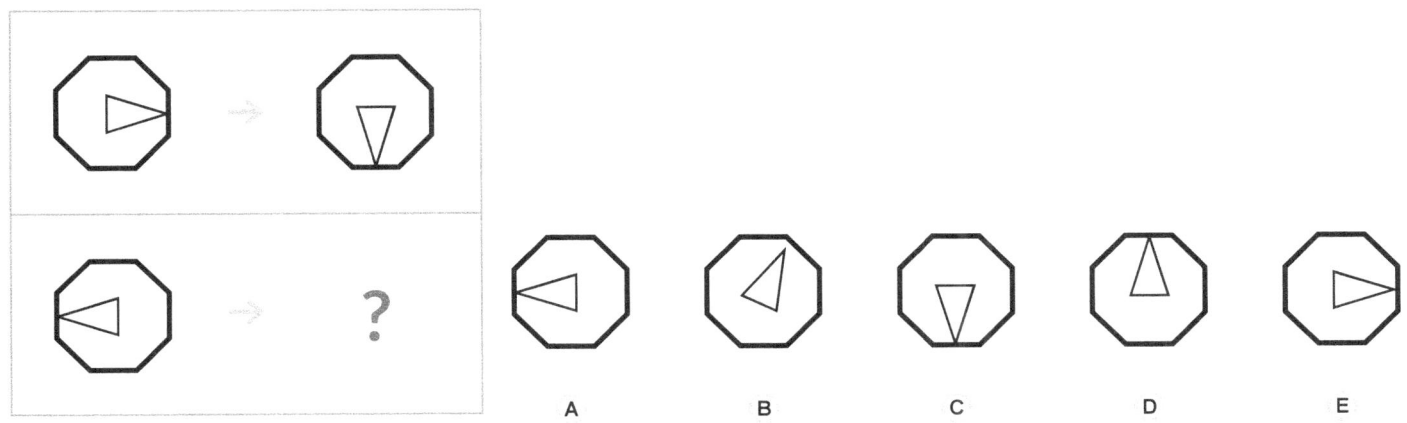

A   B   C   D   E

5

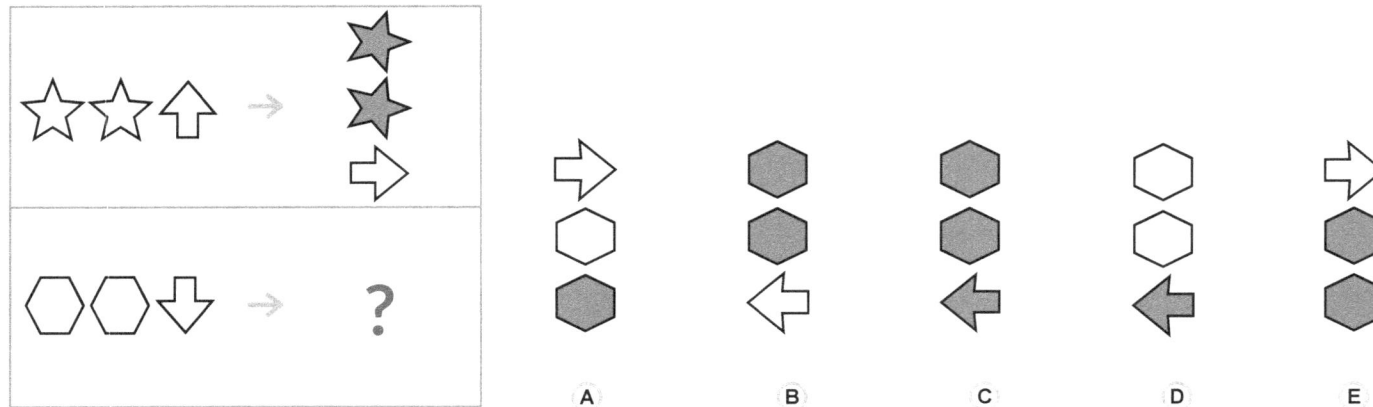

6

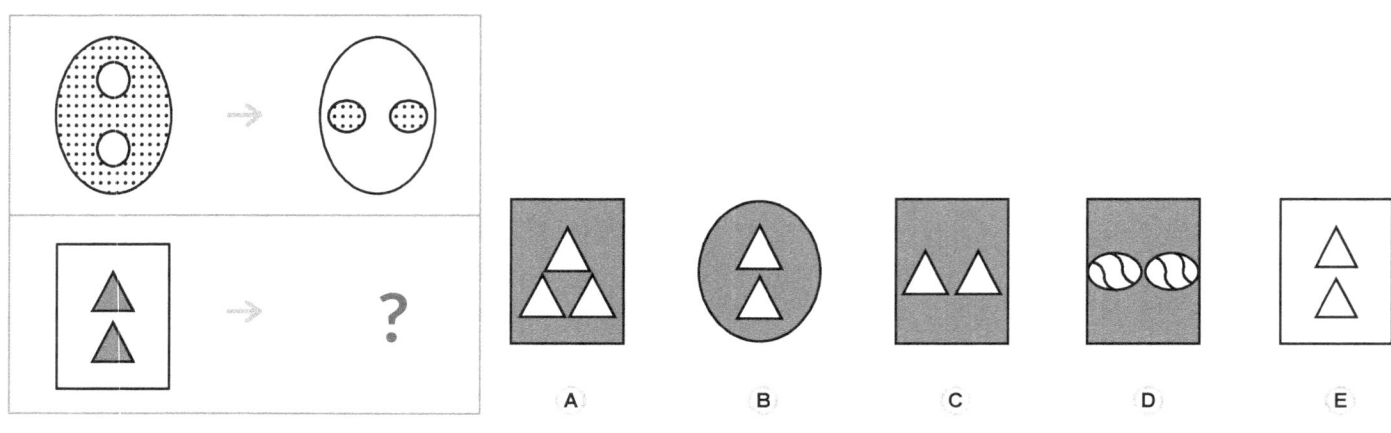

7

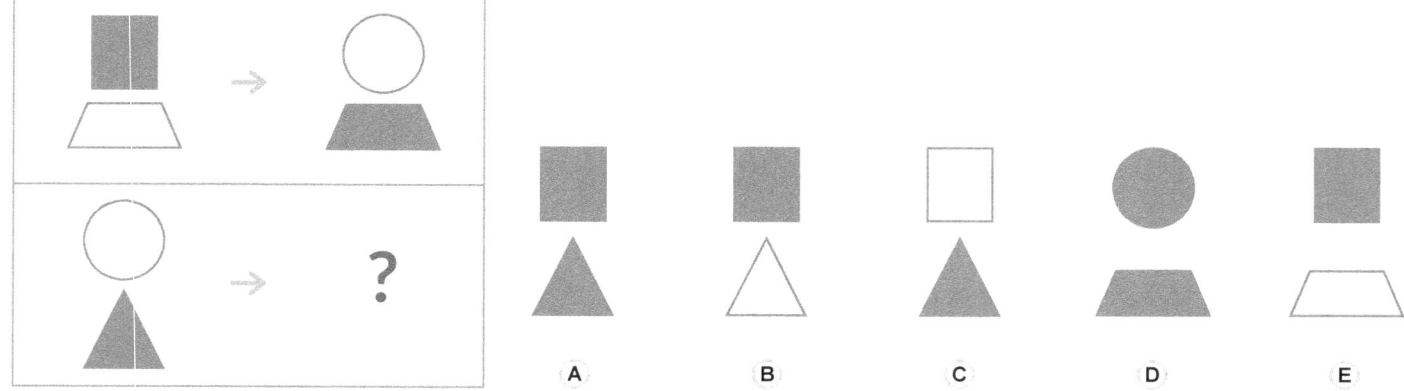

8

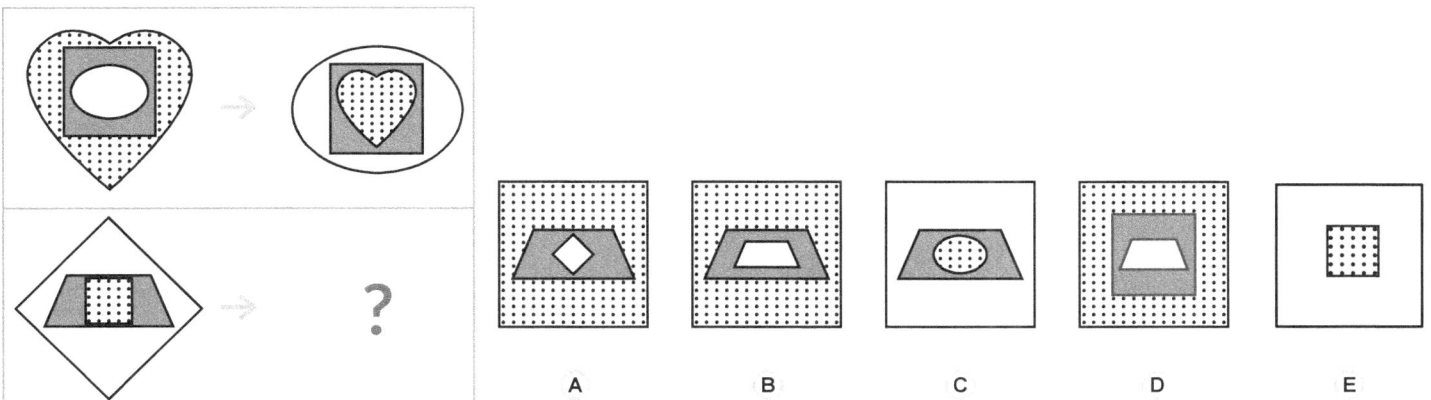

A   B   C   D   E

9

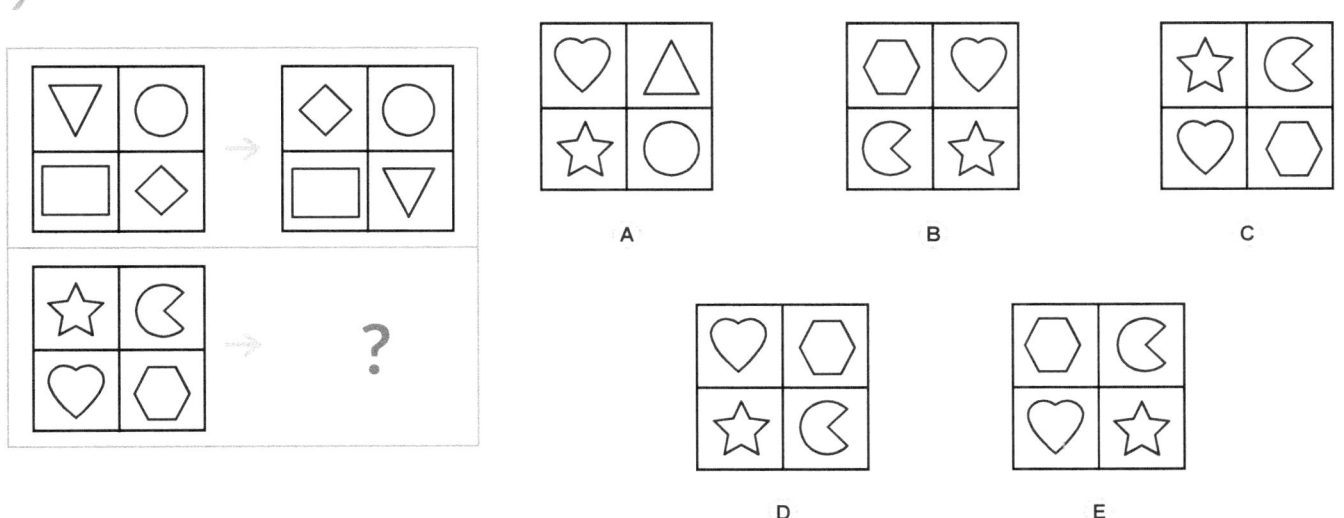

A   B   C

D   E

10

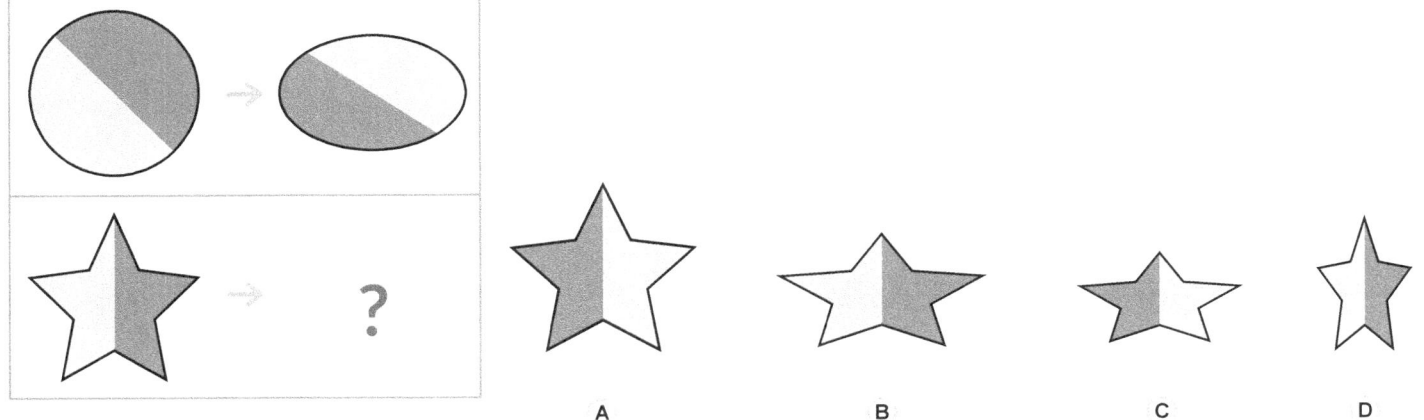

A   B   C   D

11

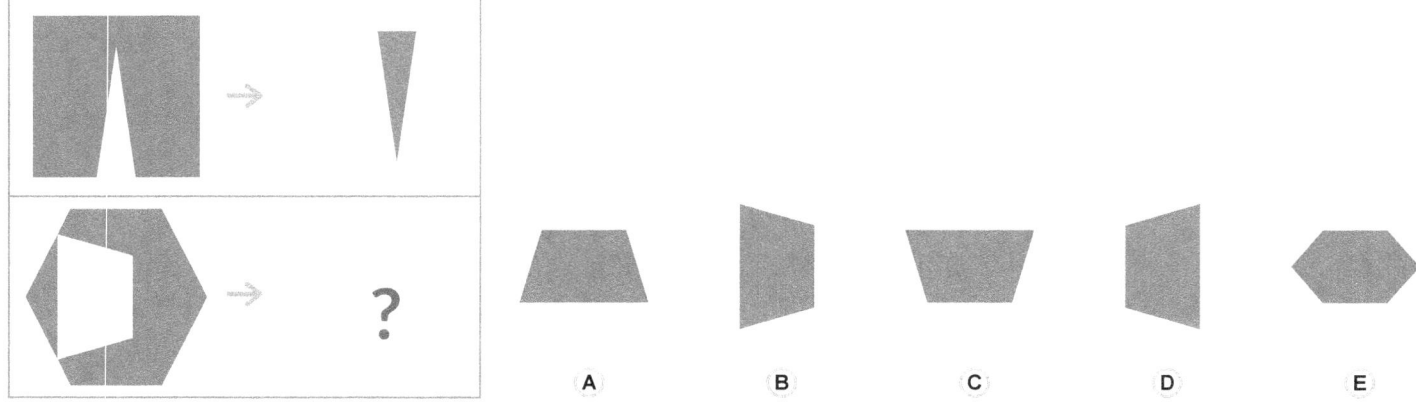

12

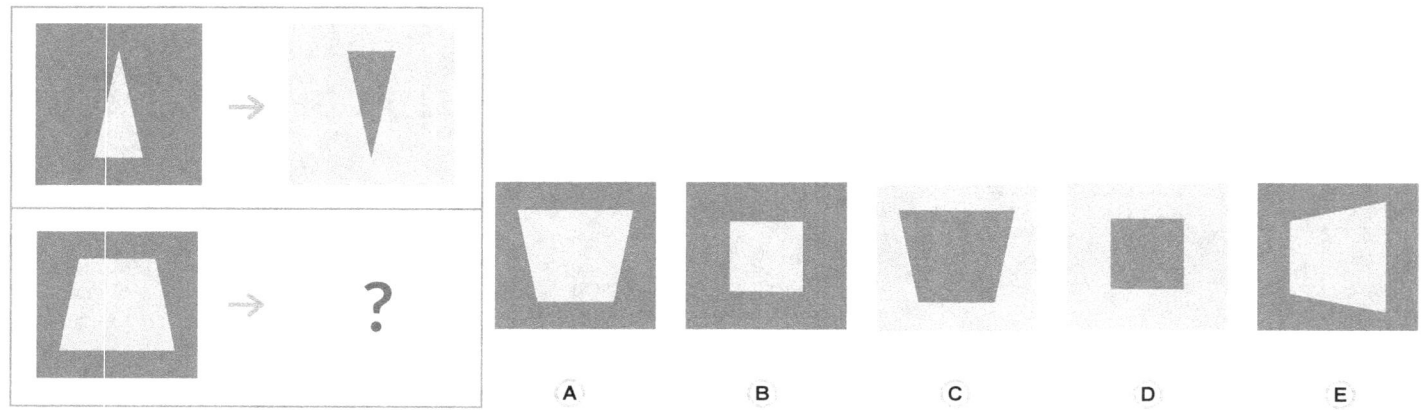

13

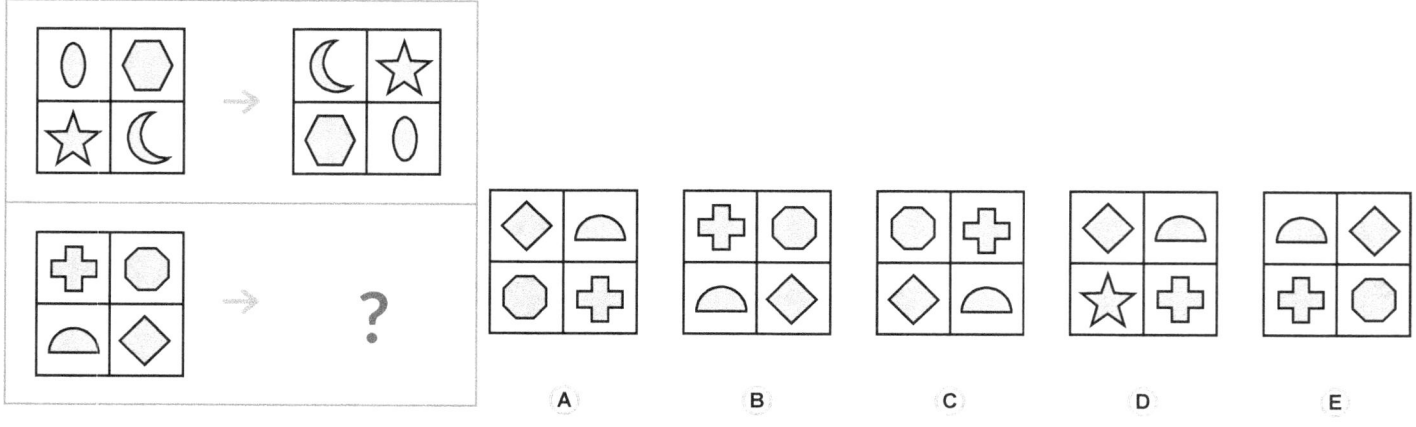

18

14

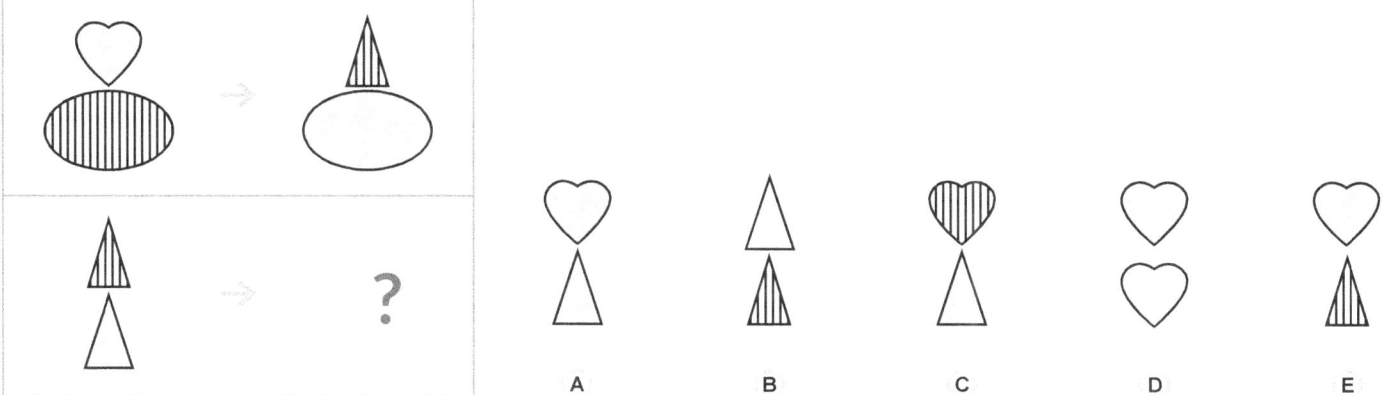

15

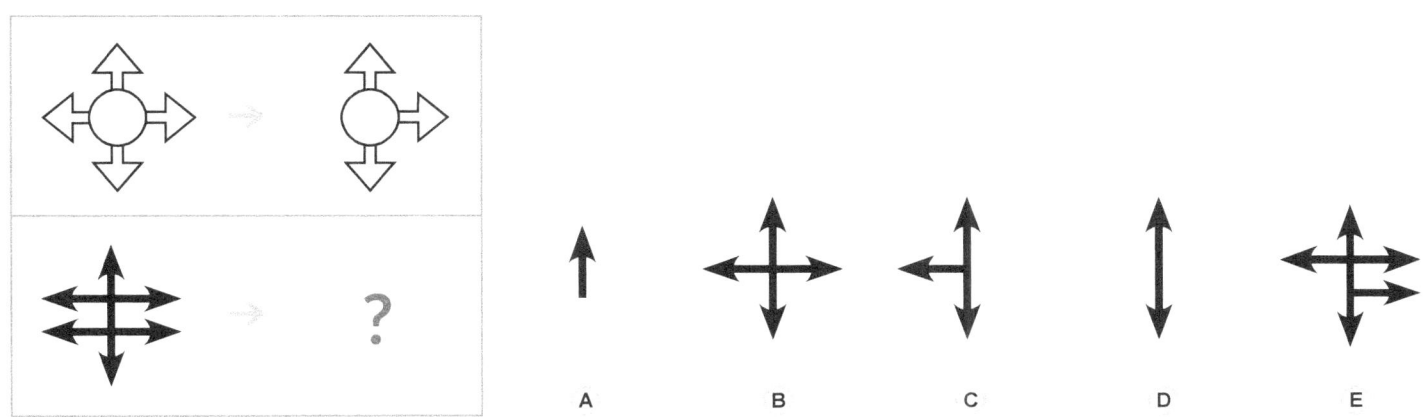

16

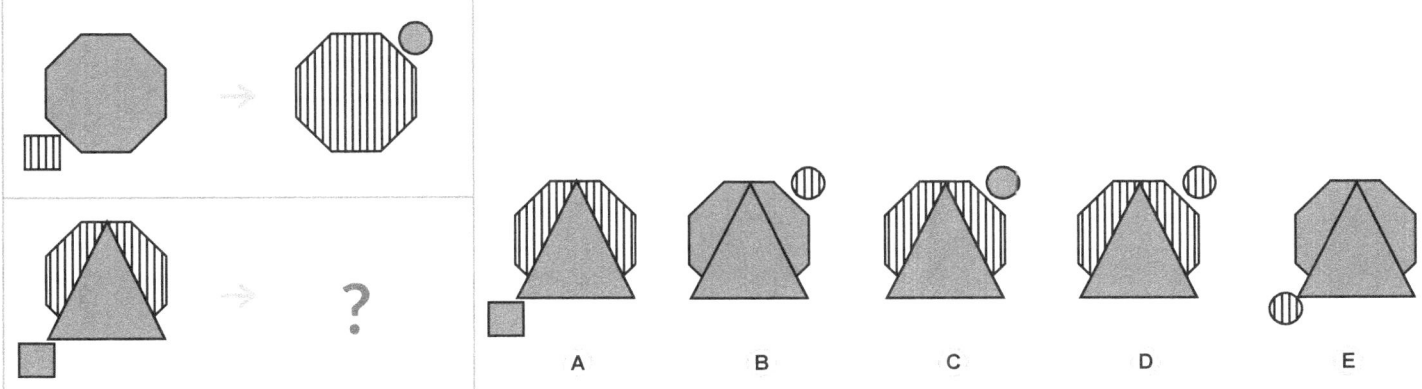

17

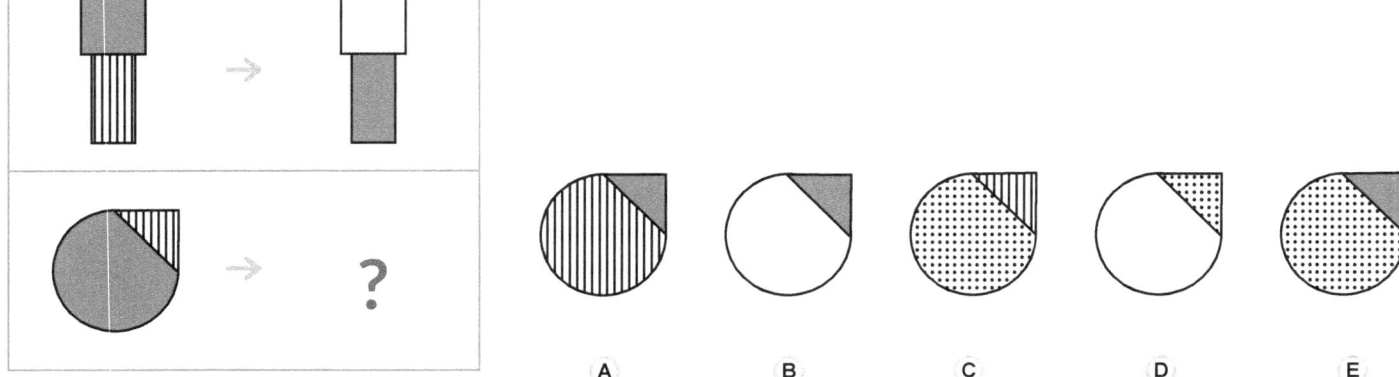

18

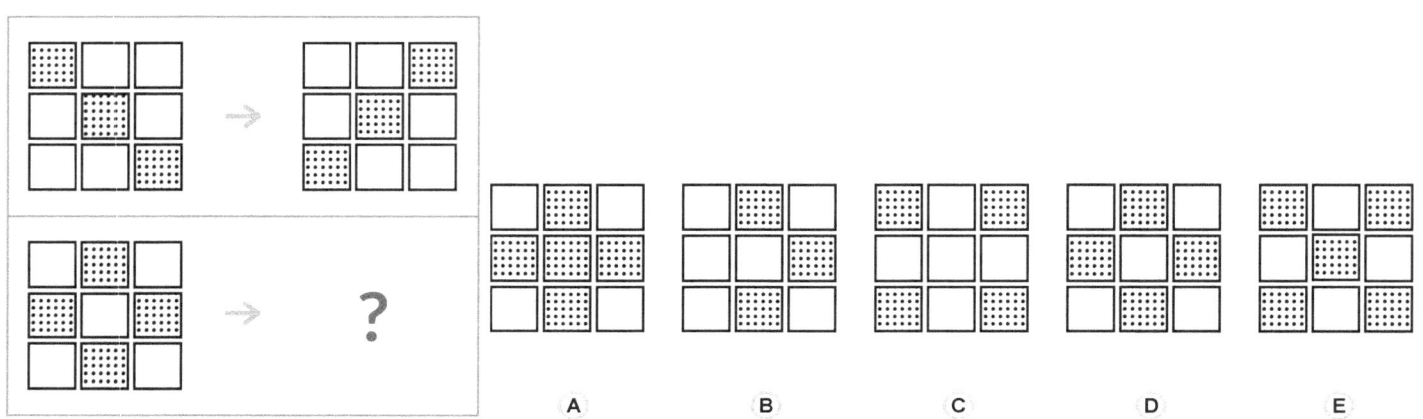

19

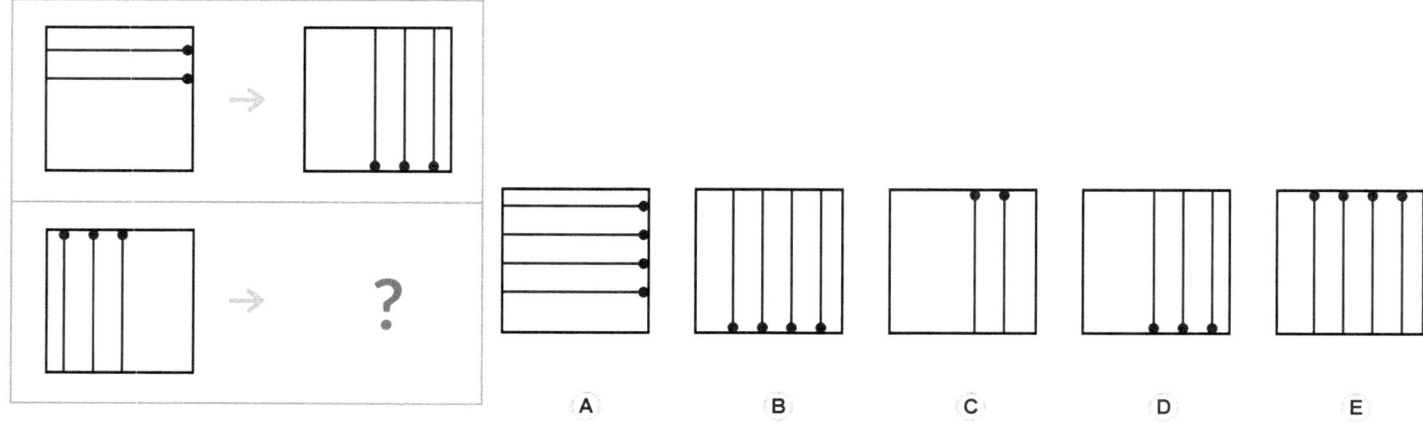

FIGURE CLASSIFICATION

What picture on the bottom goes best with those on top?

Kai

Directions: The top row shows three pictures that are alike in some way. Look at the bottom row. There are five pictures. Which picture in the bottom row goes best with the pictures in the top row?

Explanation (for parents): A more detailed explanation of Figure Classification questions is on p.8. If you have not already, look over p. 8. Following is an excerpt.

Together with your child, try to figure out a "rule" describing how the top pictures are alike and belong together. Then, apply the "rule" to each answer choice to determine which one follows it.

If your child finds that more than one choice follows the rule, then a more specific rule is needed.

The "rule" for number 1 would be "the shape is gray." The shapes are different kinds of shapes - an octagon, an oval, and a parallelogram. The "rule" they have in common is that they are gray. Choice B is the answer.

1

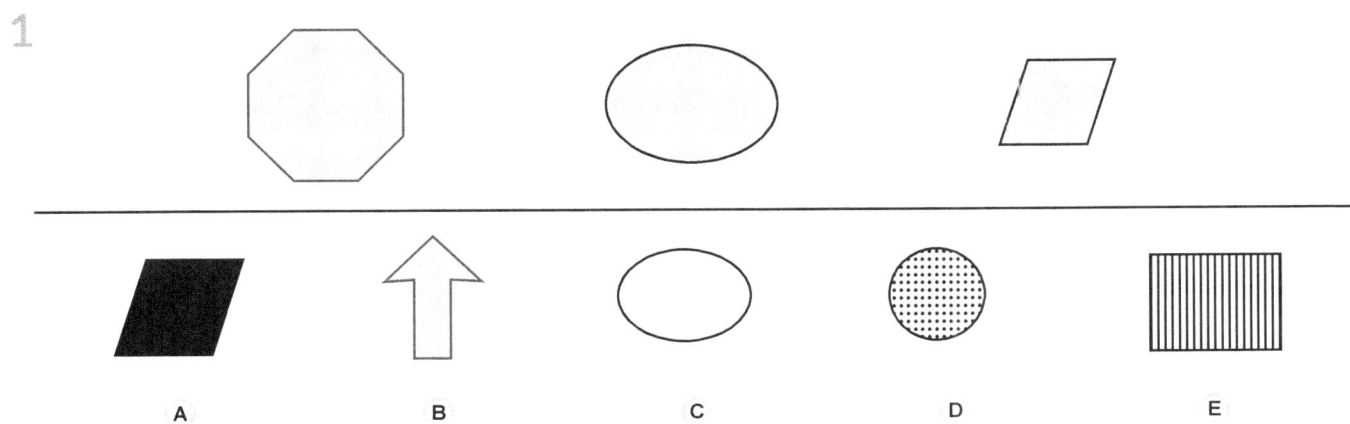

2

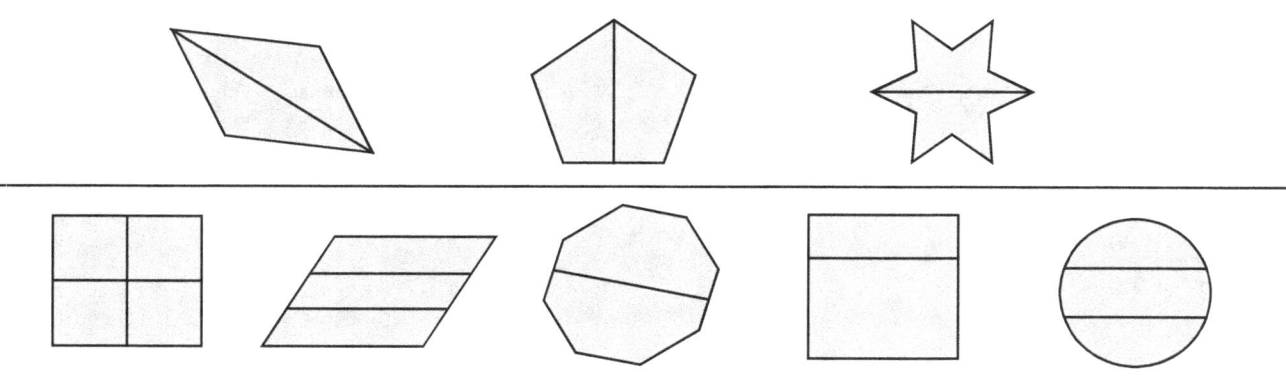

A	B	C	D	E

3

A   B   C   D   E

4

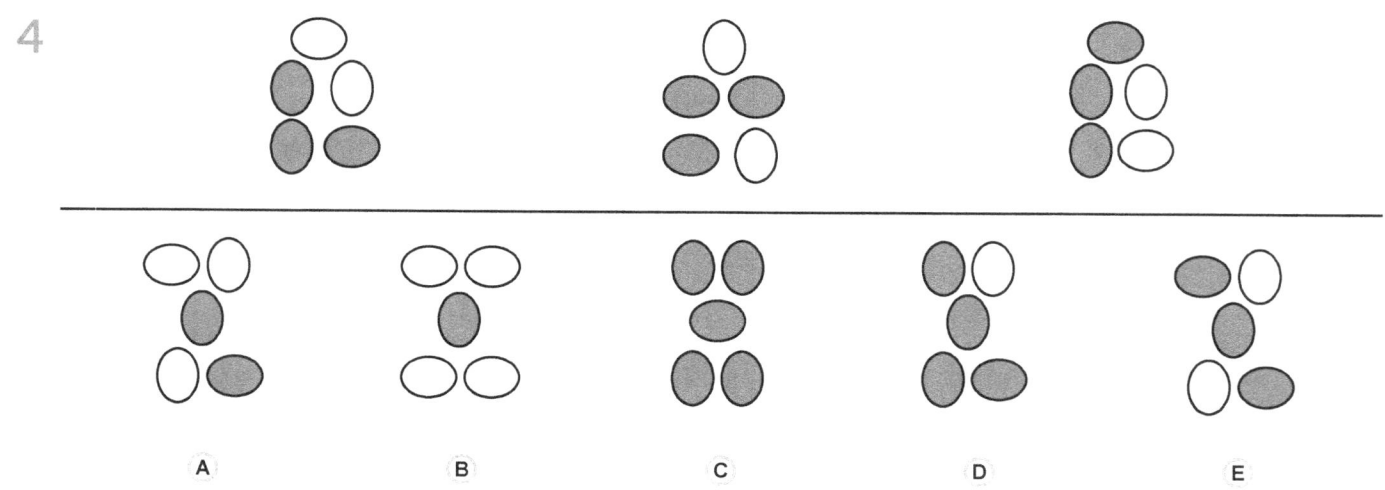

A	B	C	D	E

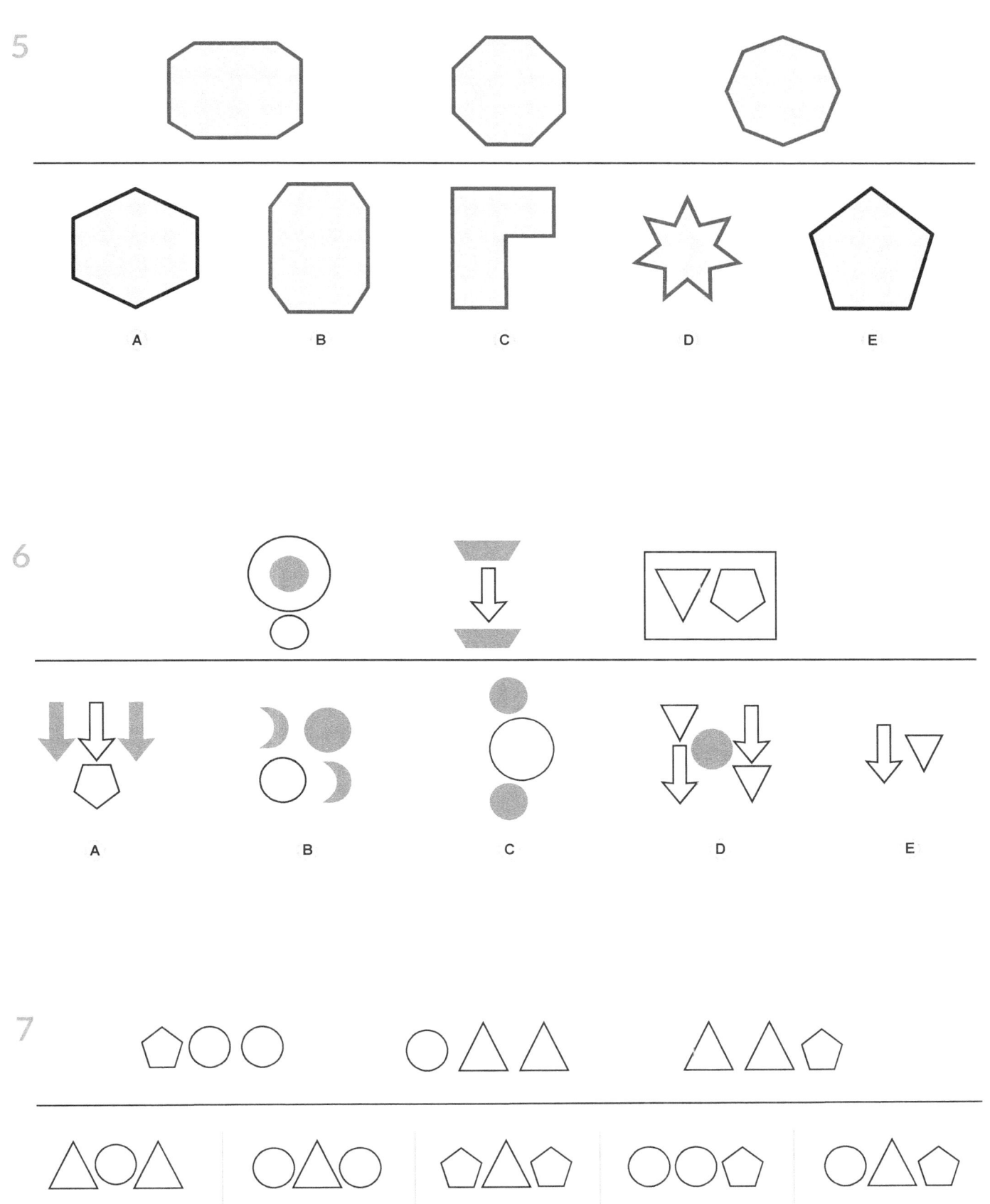

8

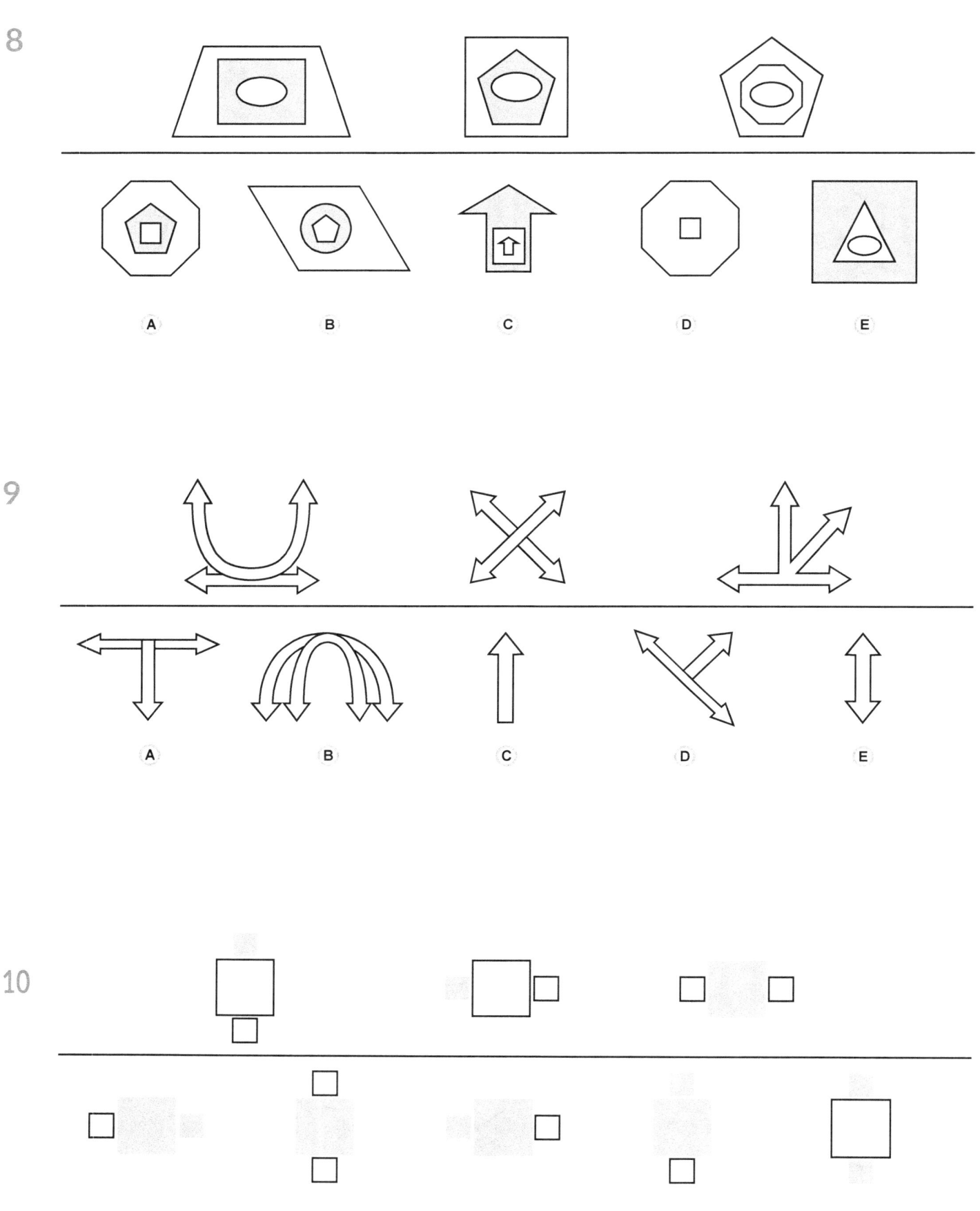

9

10

24

11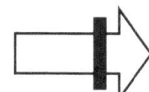

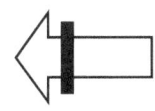 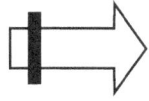 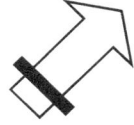  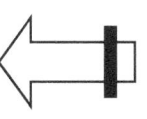

A   B   C   D   E

12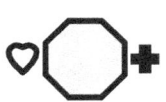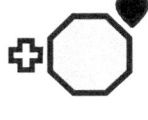

A   B   C   D   E

13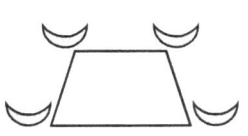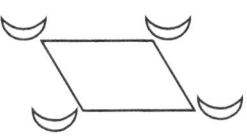

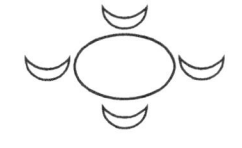  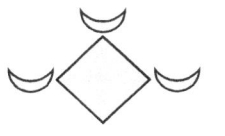

A   B   C   D   E

14

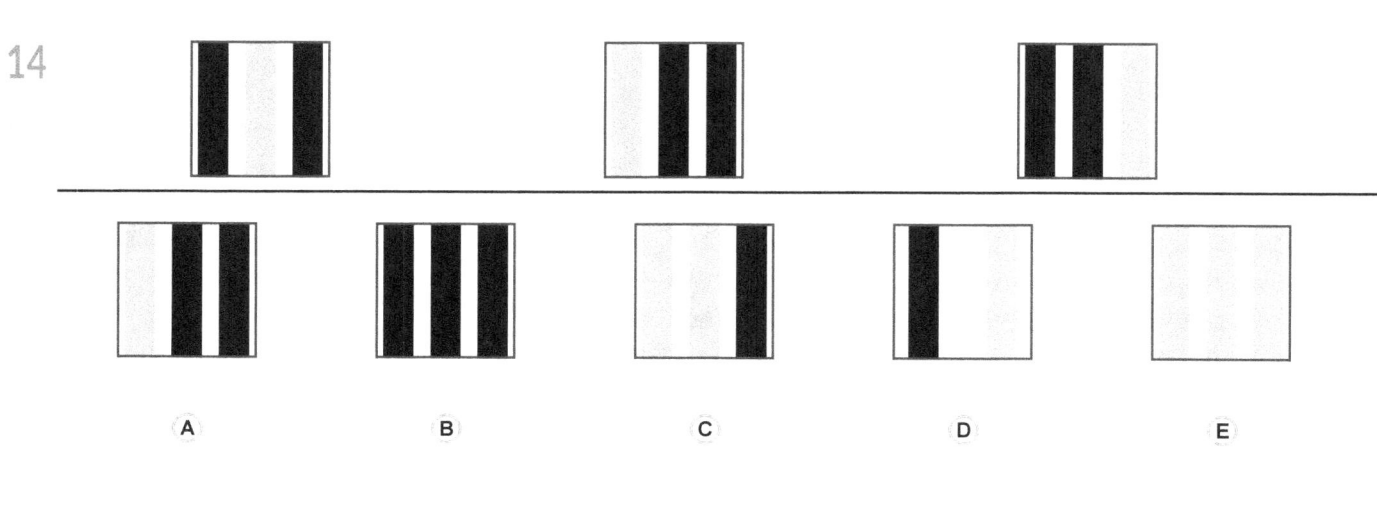

15

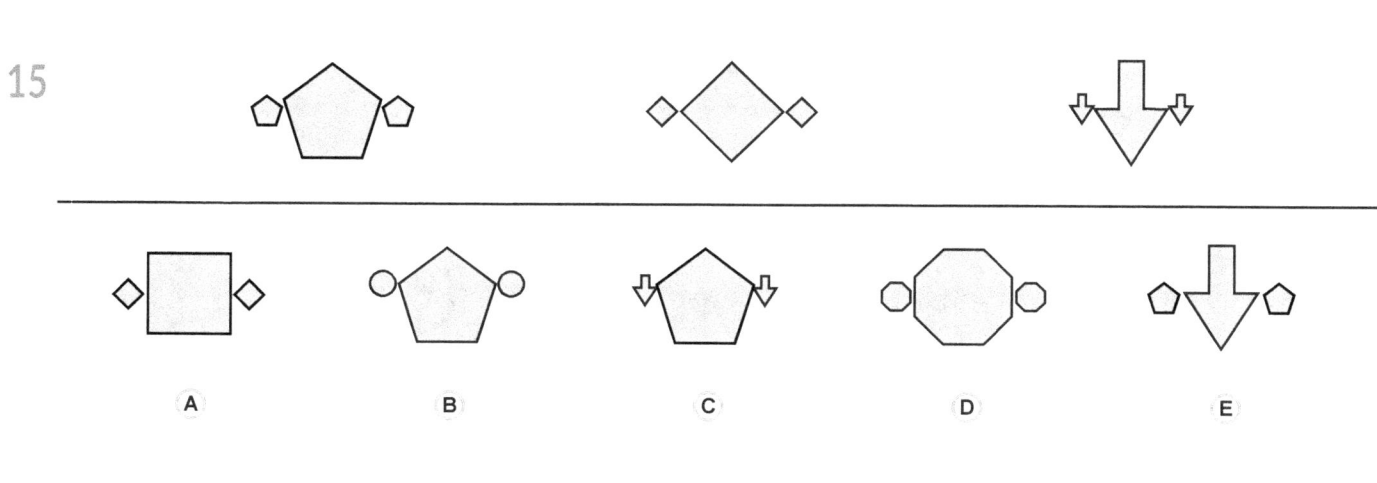

16

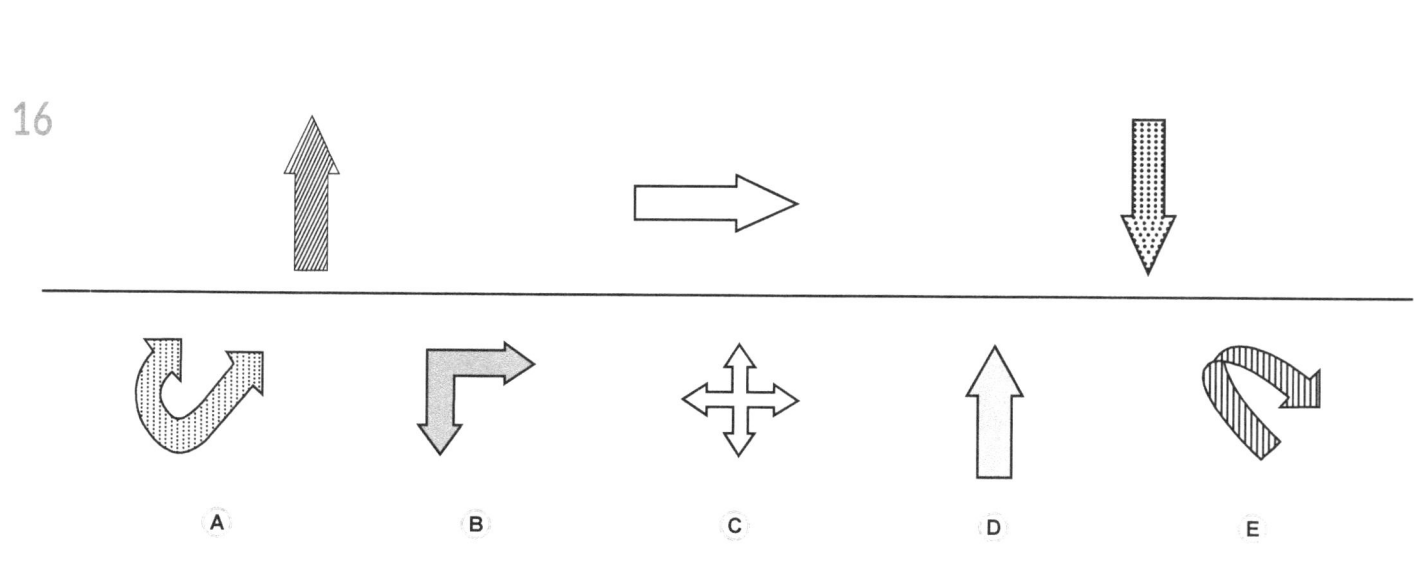

17

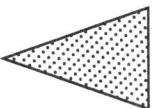 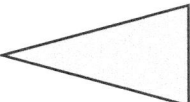 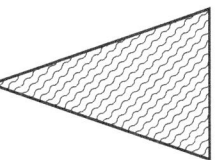

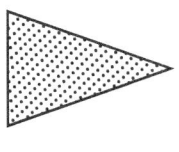 

A   B   C   D   E

18

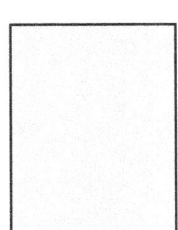 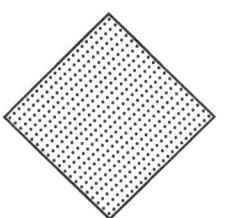 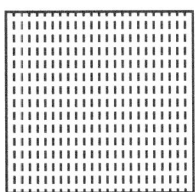

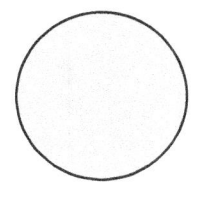  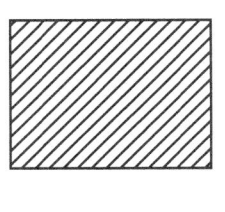 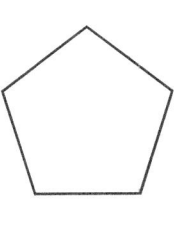 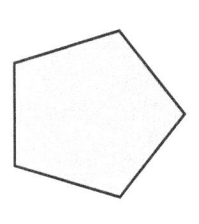

A   B   C   D   E

19

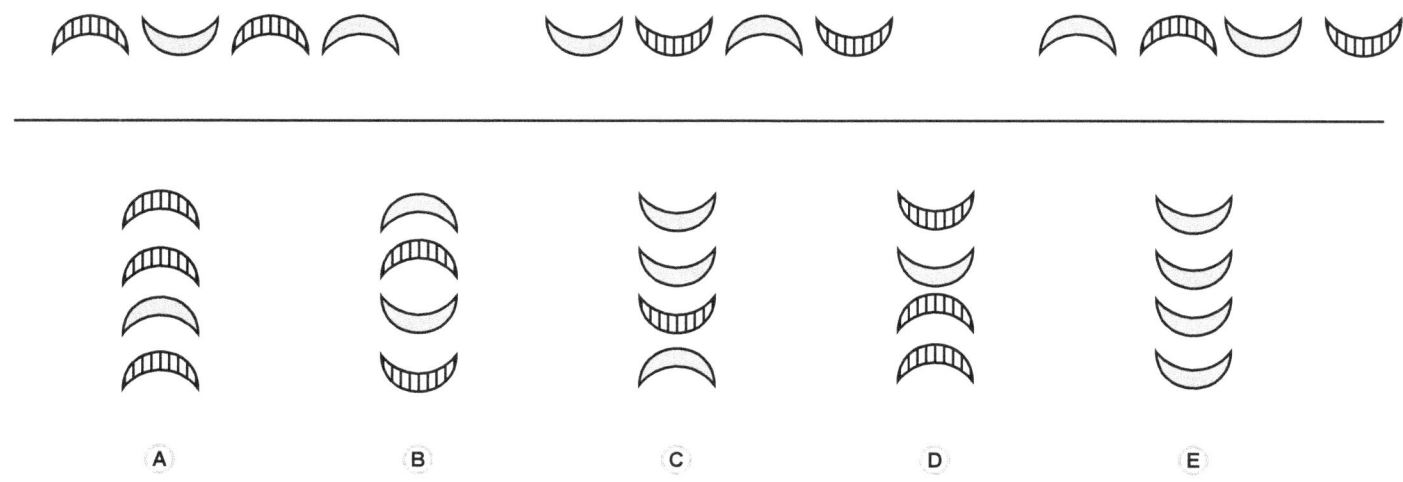

20

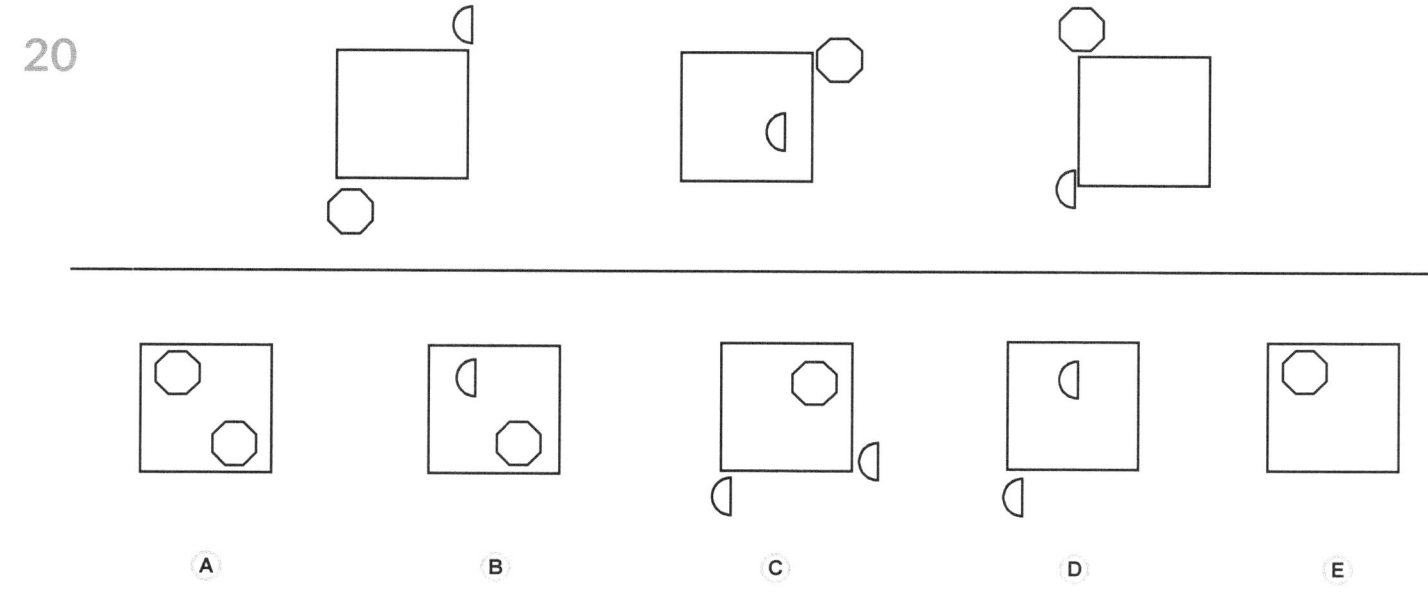

PAPER FOLDING

Look closely!

Maya

Directions: The top row of pictures shows a sheet of paper.
The paper was folded, then something was cut out. Which picture in the bottom row shows how the paper would look after it's unfolded?

Additional information (for parents): As explained earlier on p. 11, children may initially be "stumped" by Paper Folding. If your child needs help, then try demonstrating with real paper and a hole puncher.

Be sure to point out the number of holes made and their position after opening the paper.

1.

A   B   C   D

2.

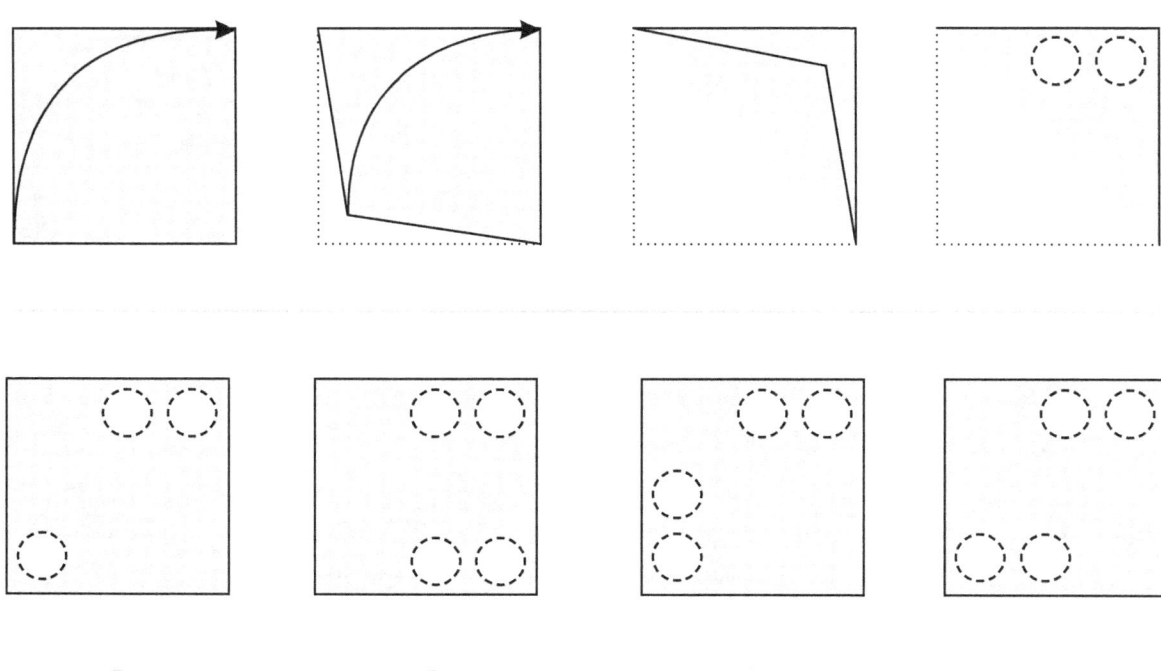

A   B   C   D

3.

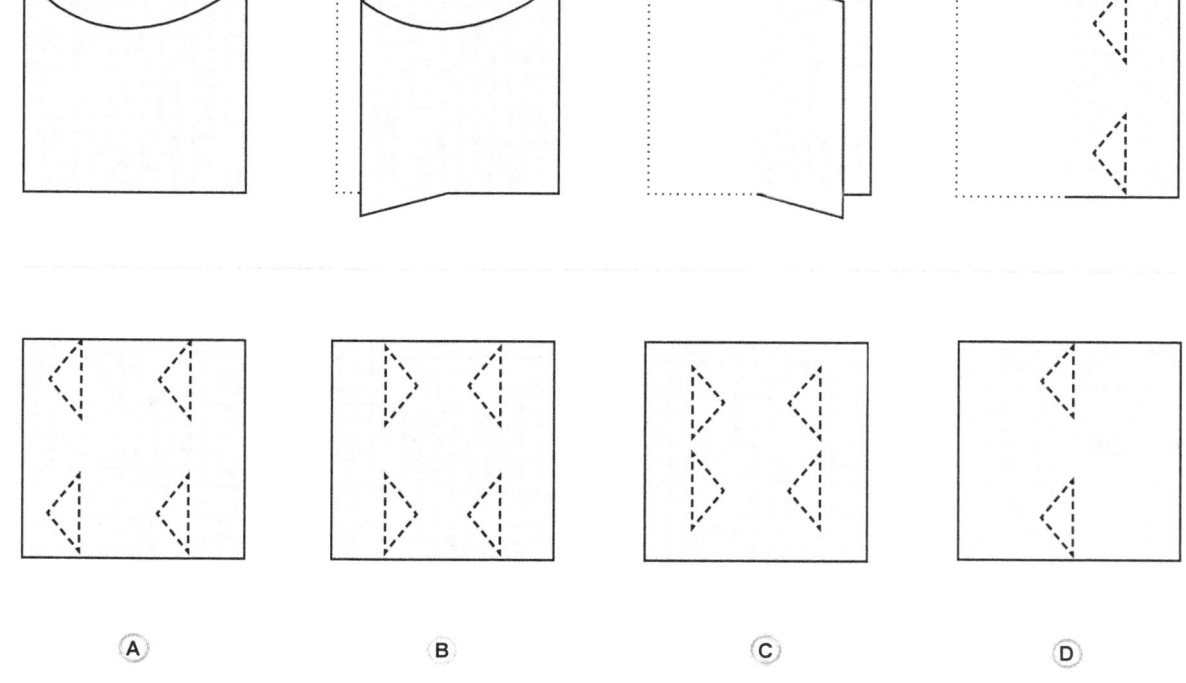

A   B   C   D

4.

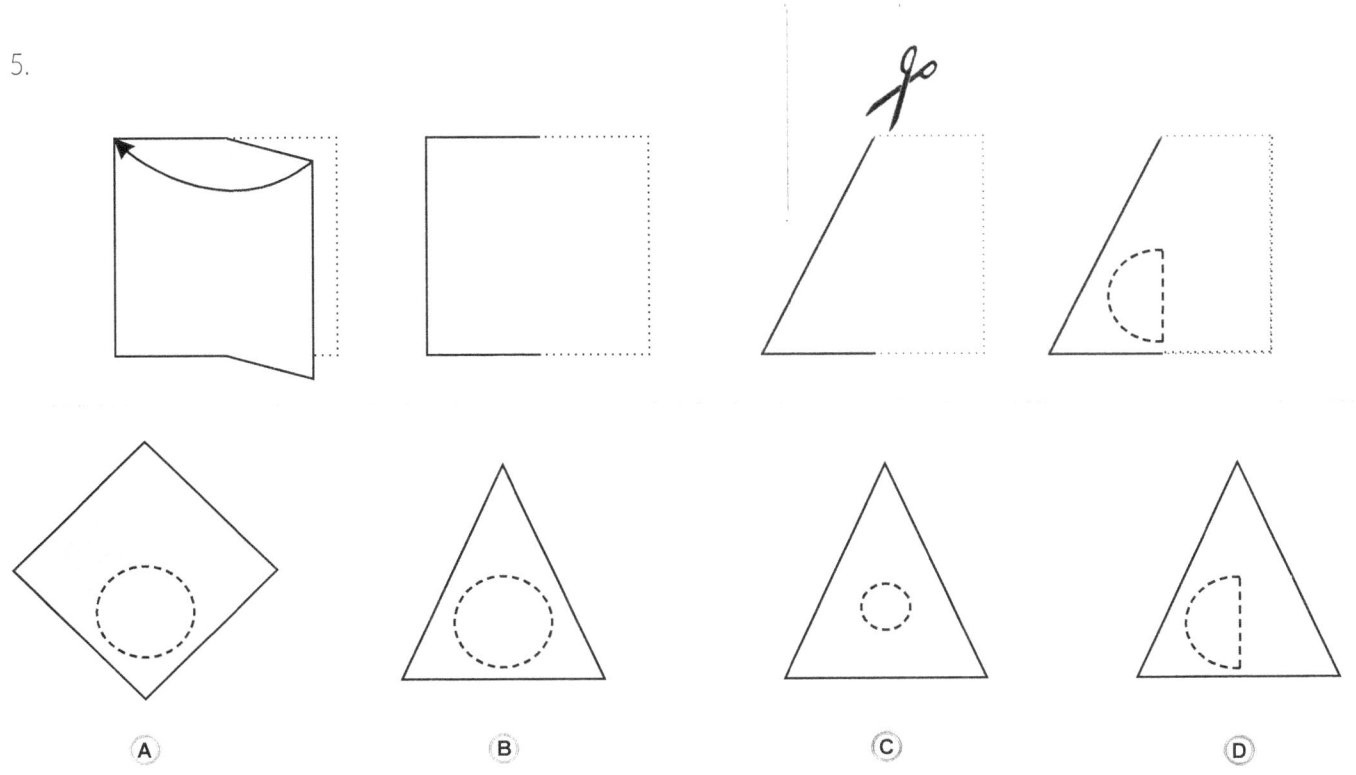

A   B   C   D

5.

A   B   C   D

Note: In the next questions, the paper is folded twice. Point this out to your child.

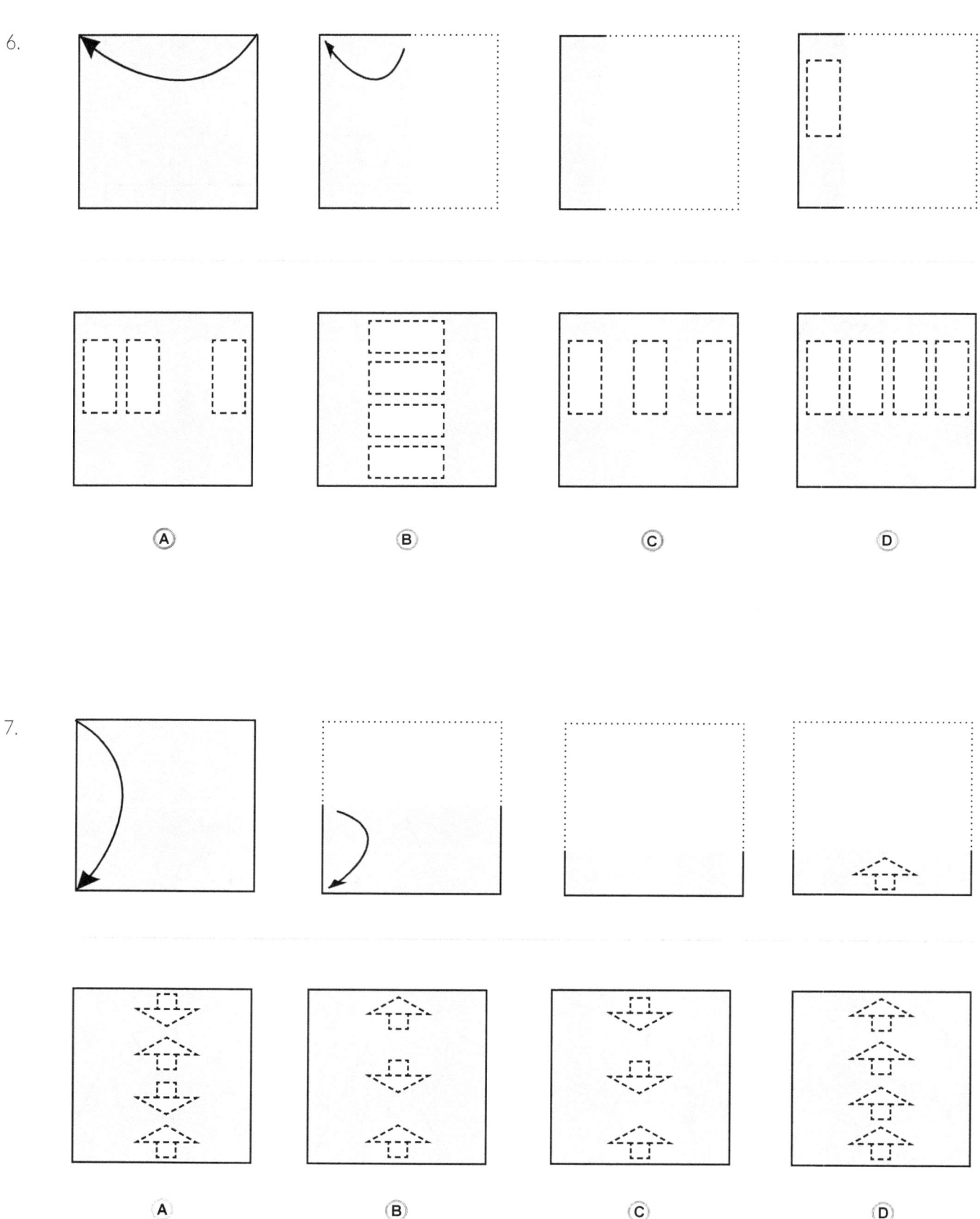

8.

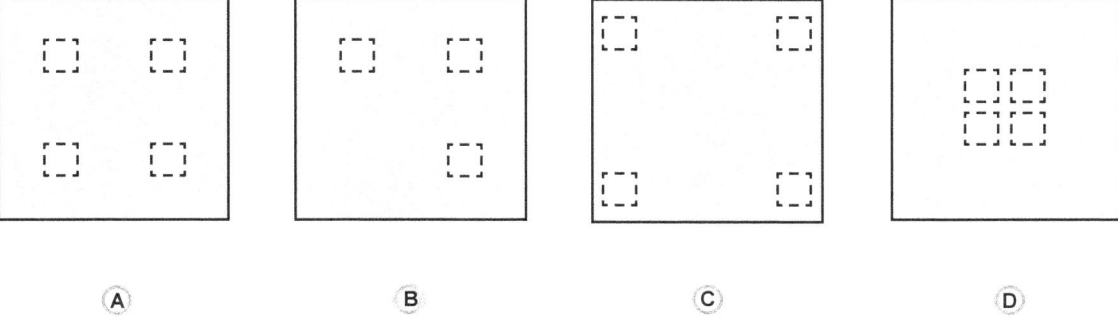

A B C D

9.

A B C D

10.

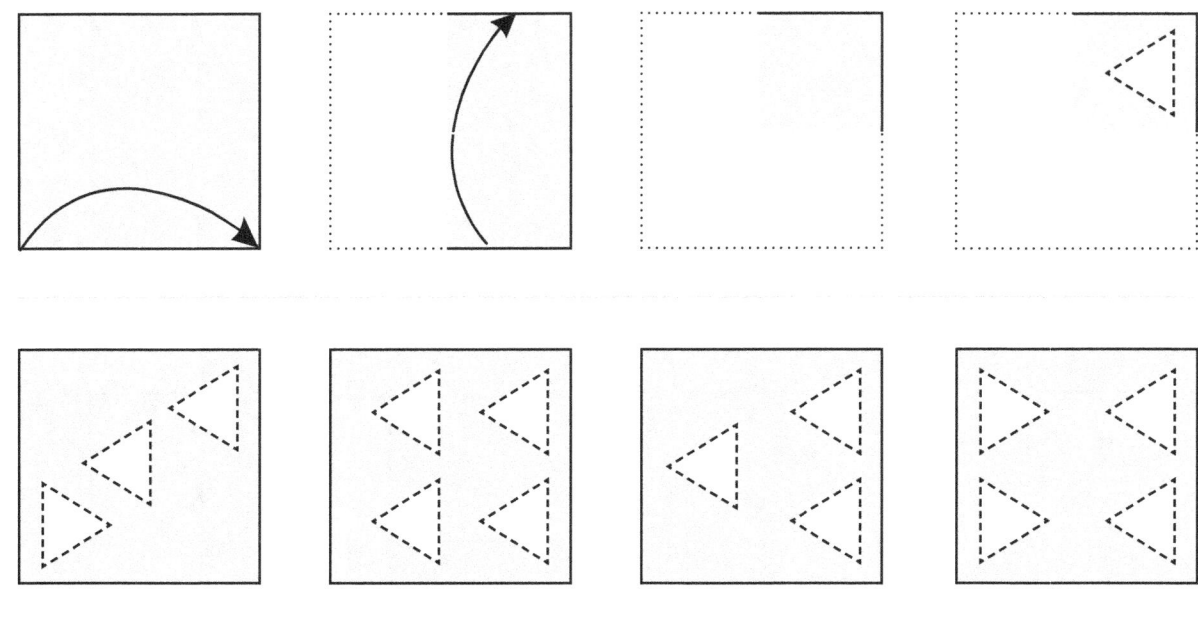

A   B   C   D

11.

A   B   C   D

12.

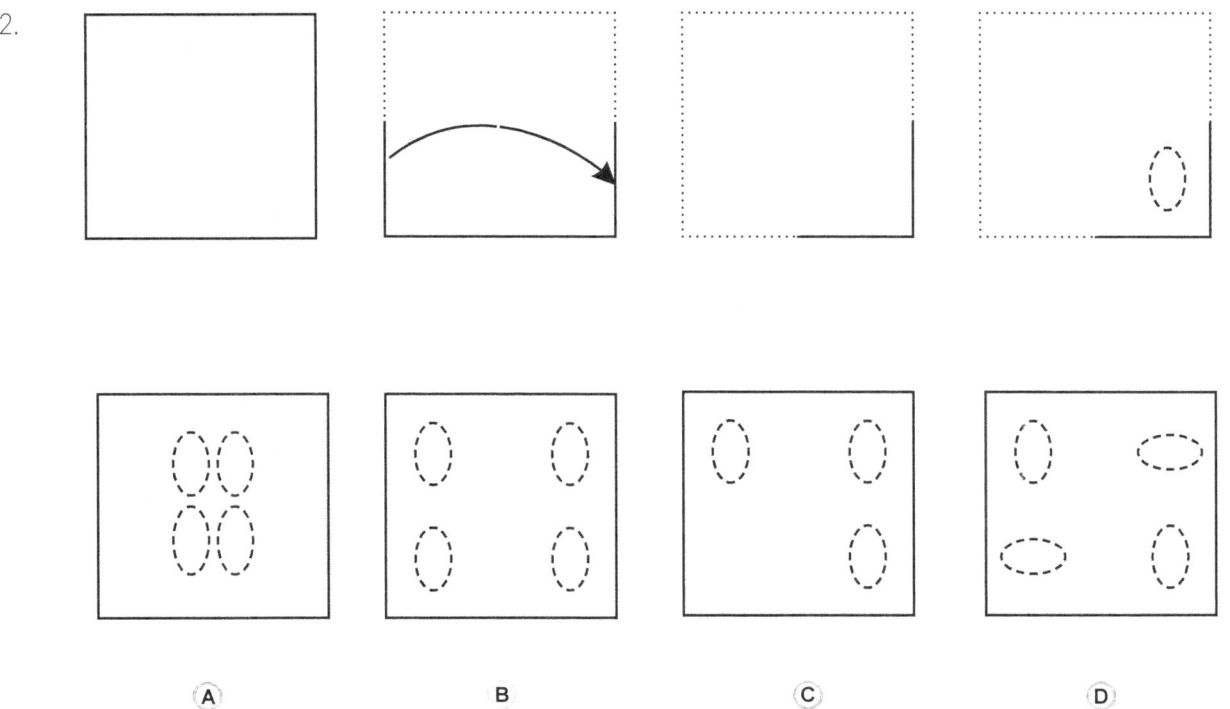

A B C D

13.

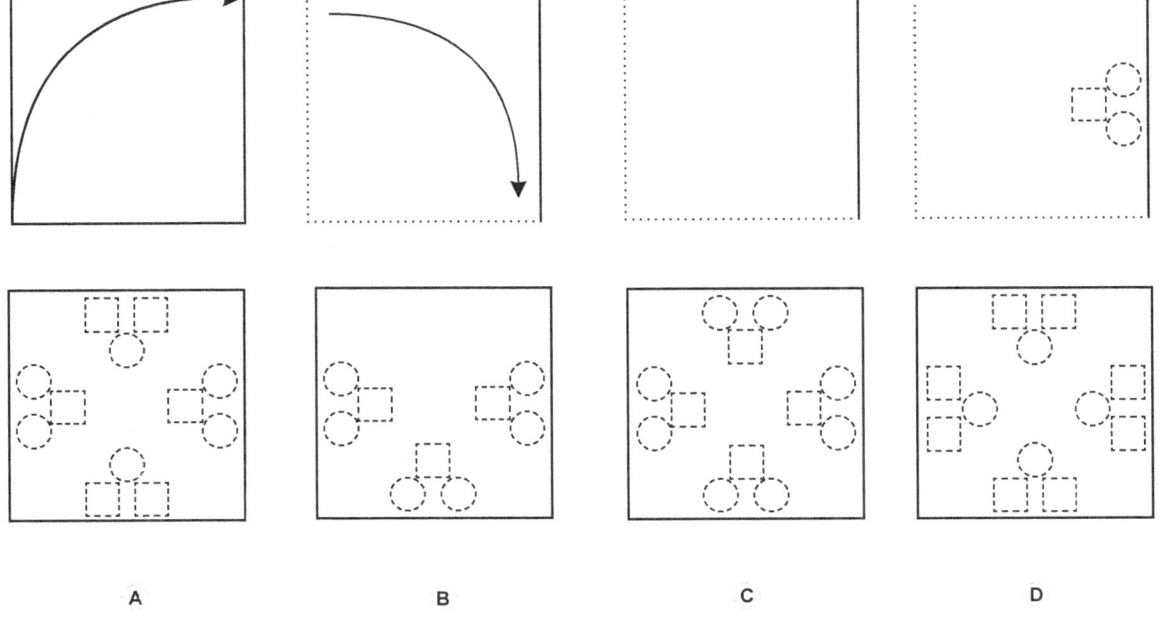

A B C D

14.

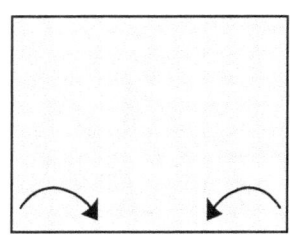 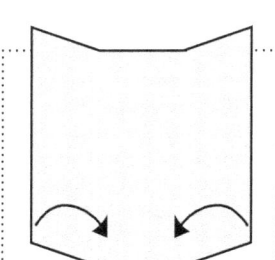  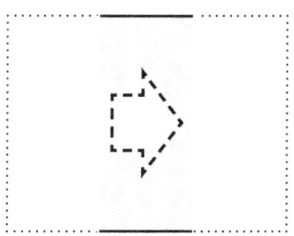

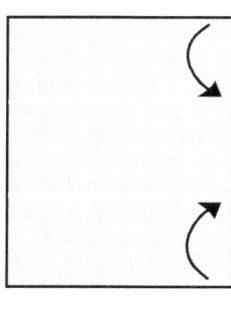 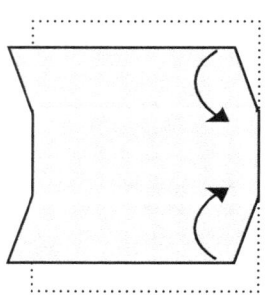  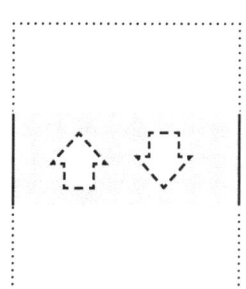

A   B   C   D

15.

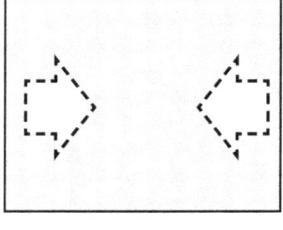 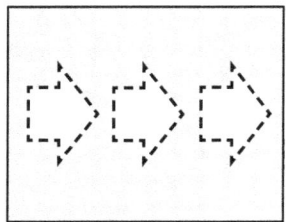 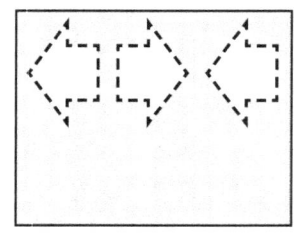

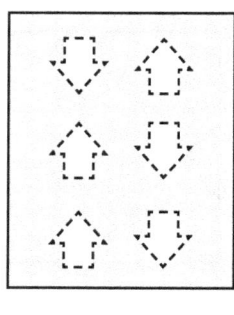 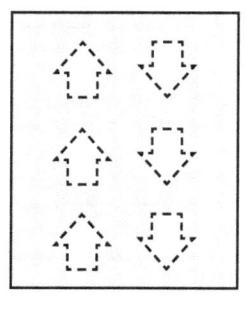 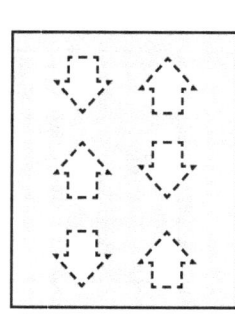

A   B   C   D

36

Zoe

- End of Practice Test 1 (Workbook Format) -
- Practice Test 2 begins on the next page. -

START OF PRACTICE TEST 2 / FIGURE ANALOGIES

Directions: The pictures in the top boxes go together in some way. One of the bottom boxes is empty. Which answer choice goes with the picture in the bottom box in the same way the top pictures do?

1

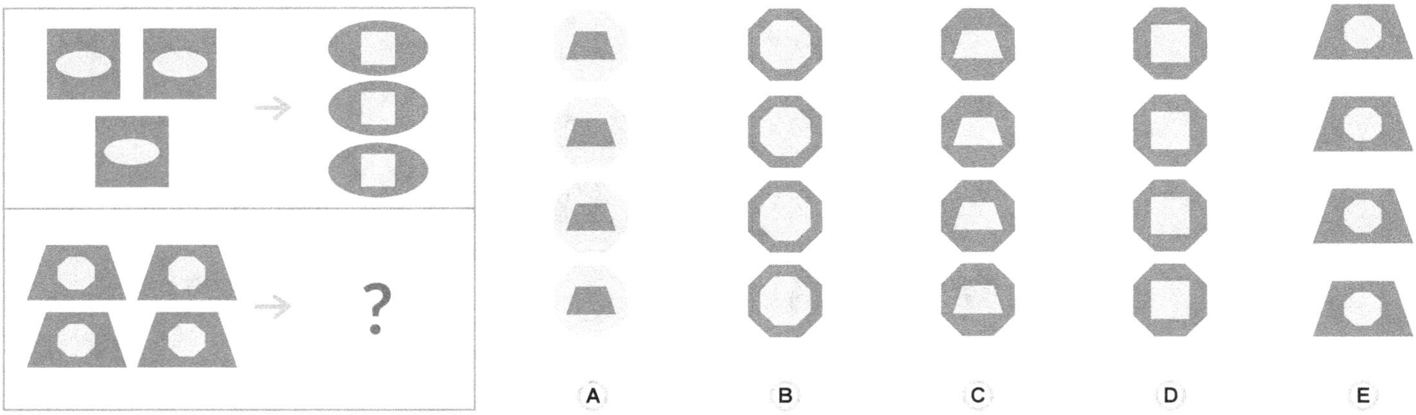

?
A
B
C
D
E

2

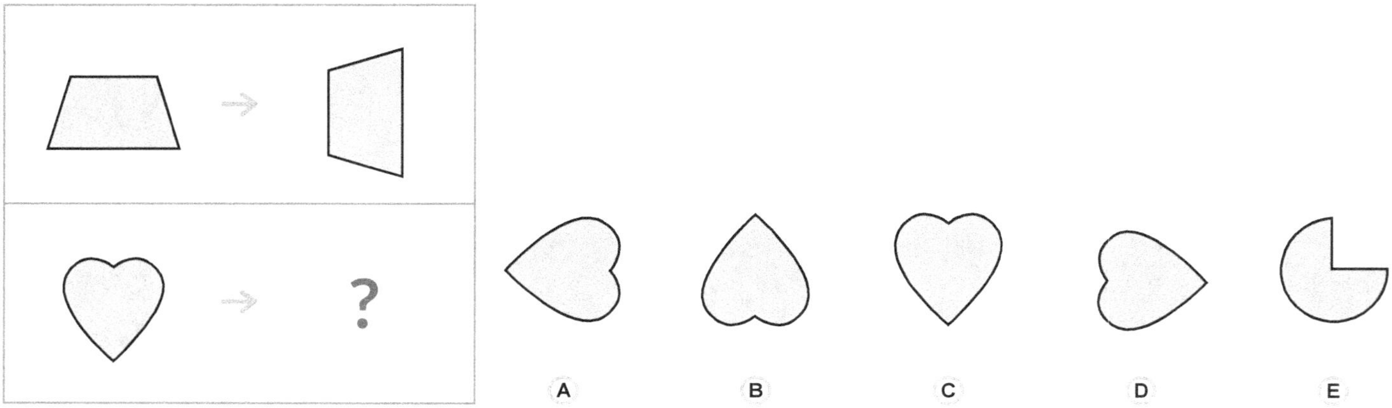

?
A
B
C
D
E

3

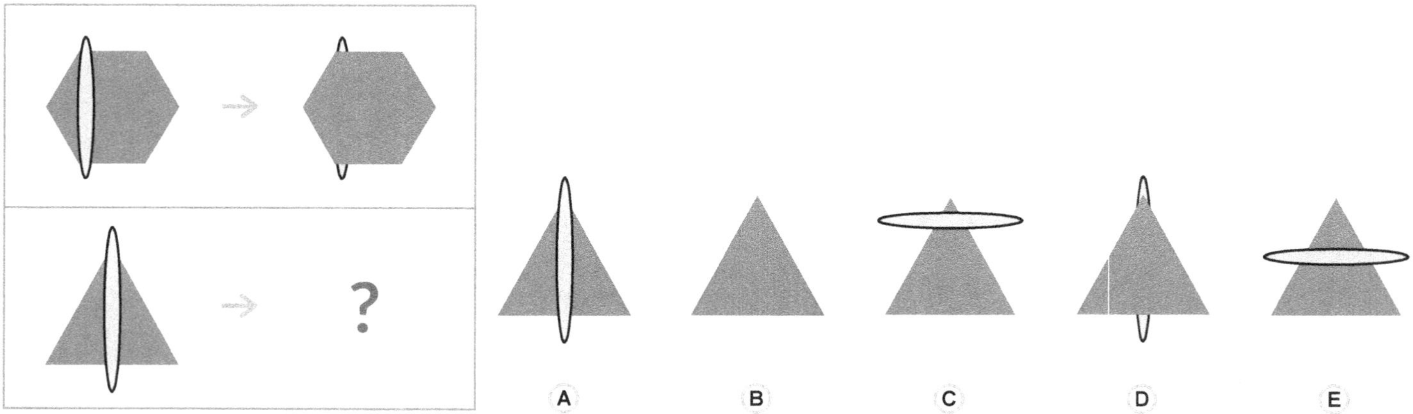

?
A
B
C
D
E

4

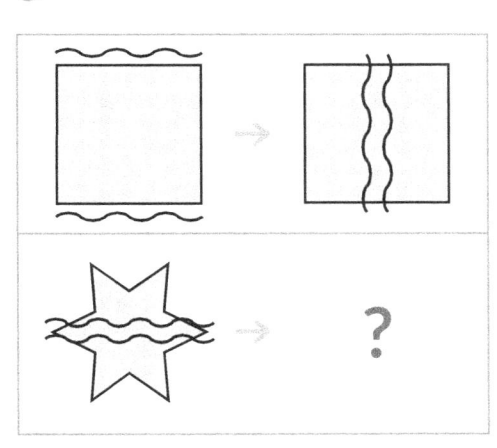

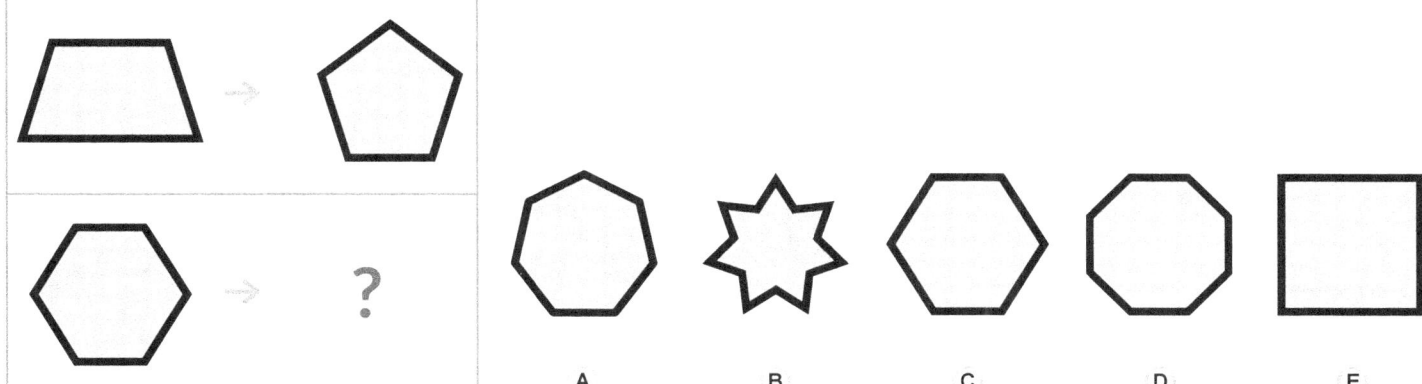

A B C D E

5

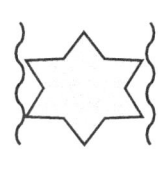

A B

 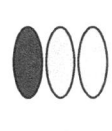 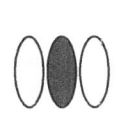

C D E

6

A B C D E

7

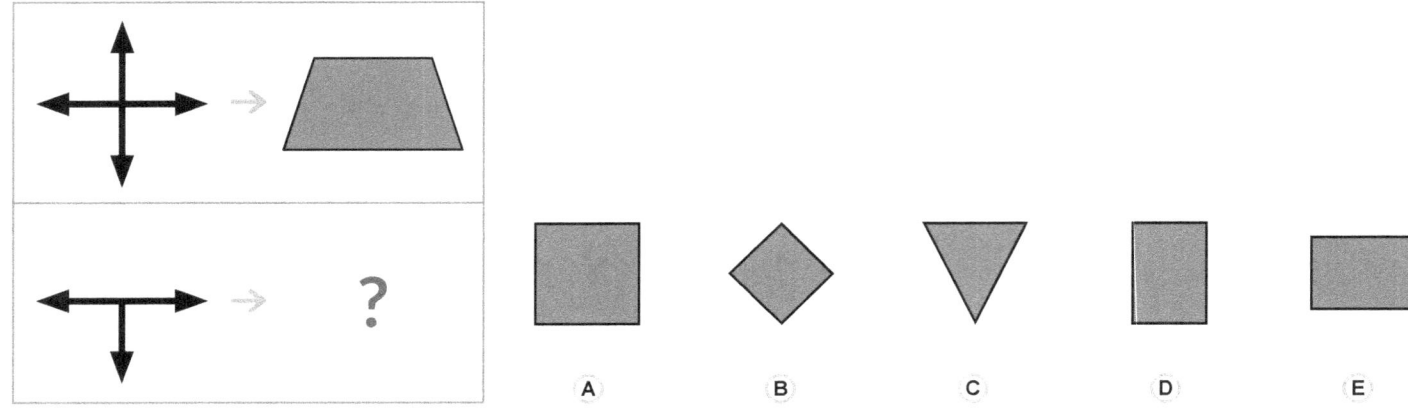

A B C D E

8

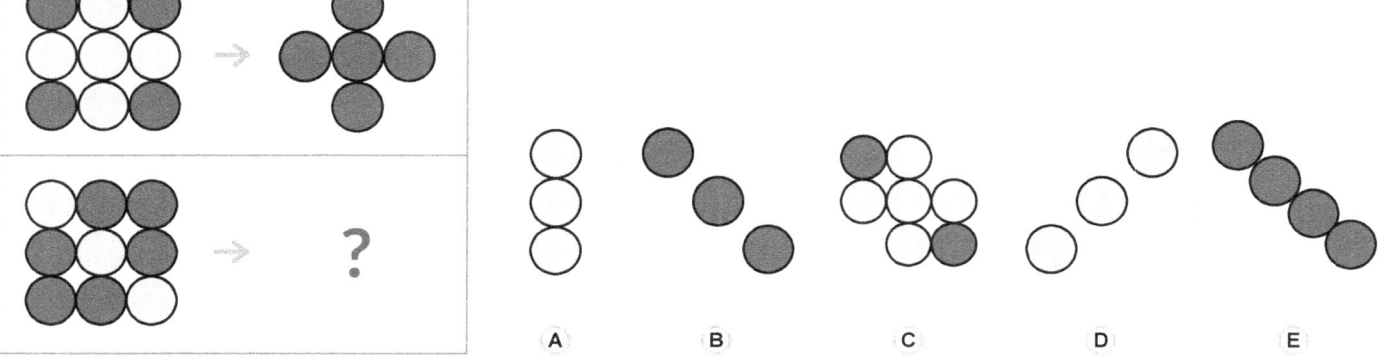

A B C D E

9

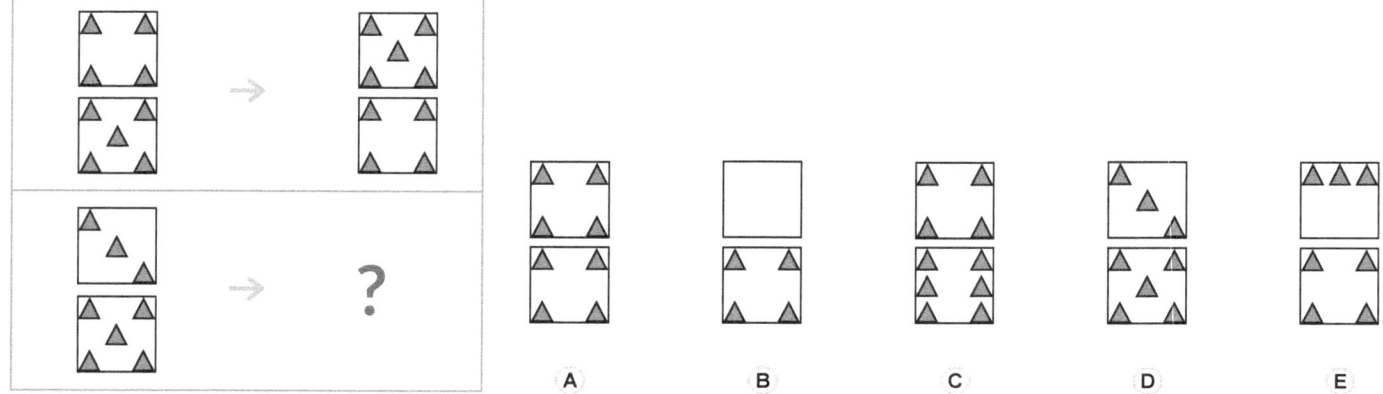

A B C D E

10

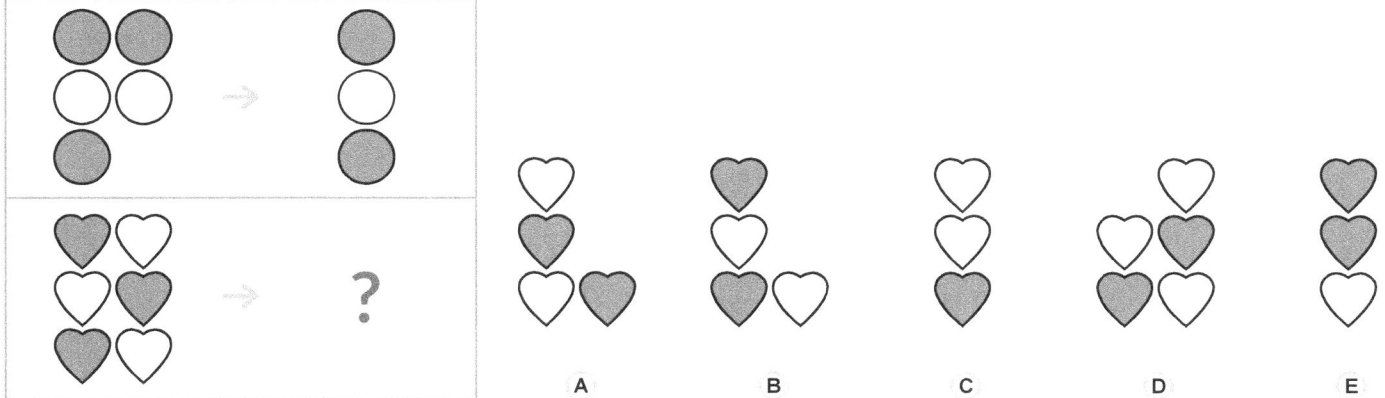

A   B   C   D   E

11

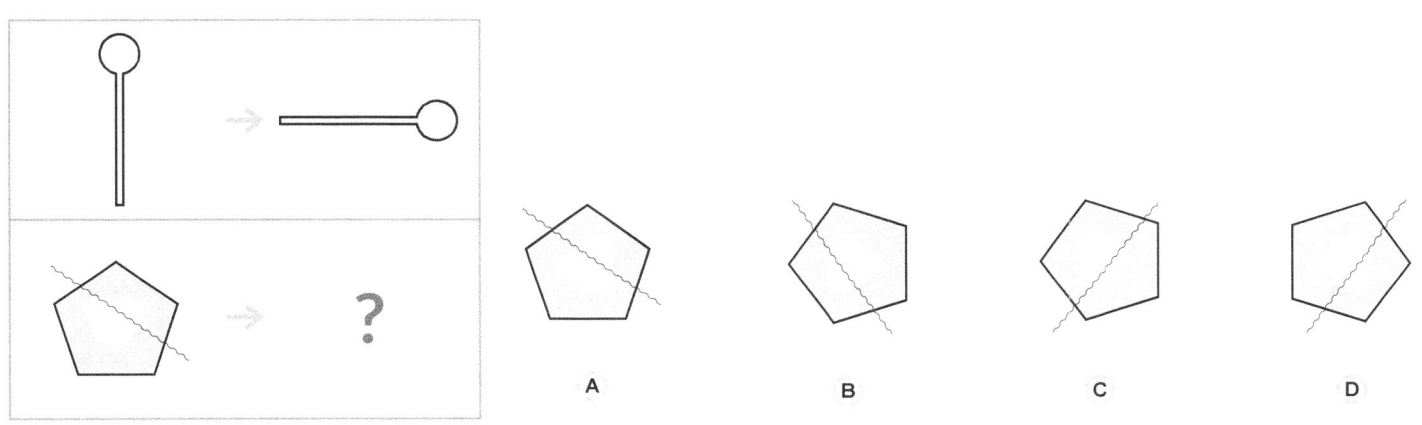

A   B   C   D

12

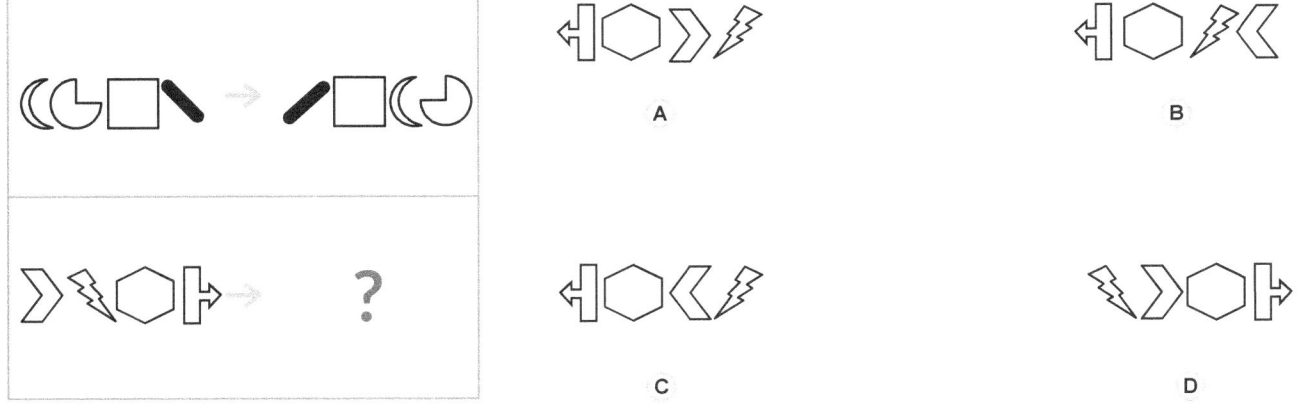

A   B

C   D

13

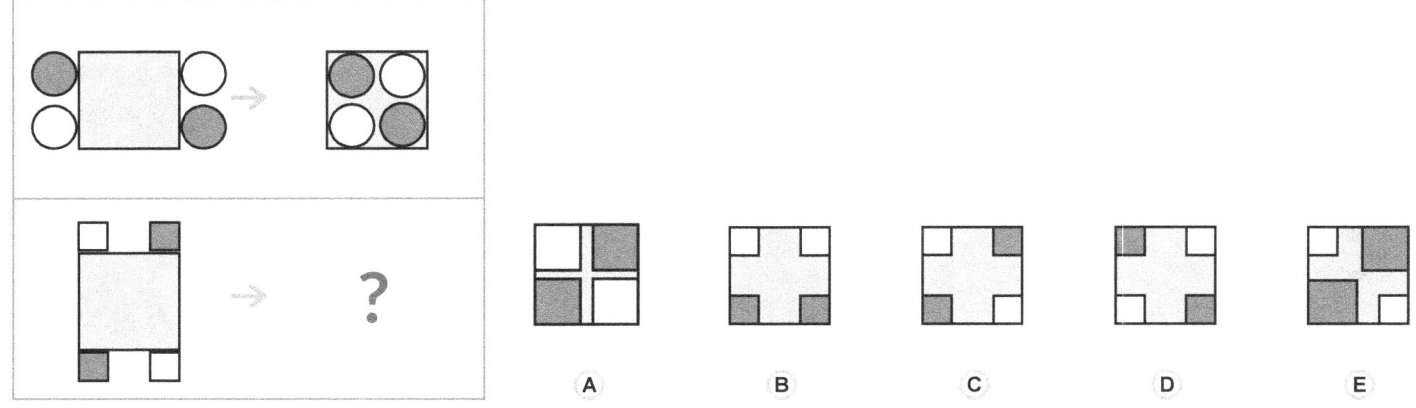

14

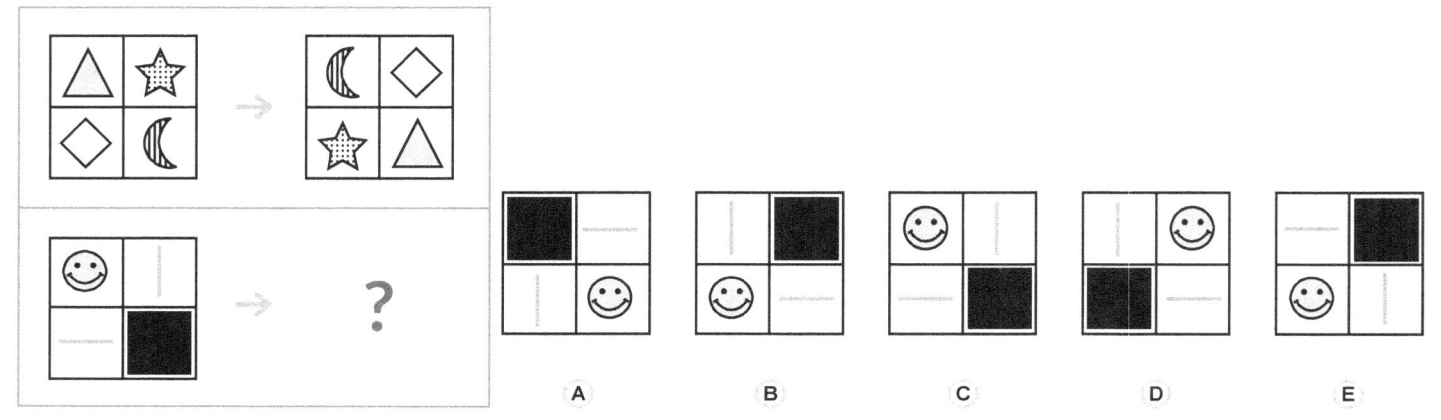

15

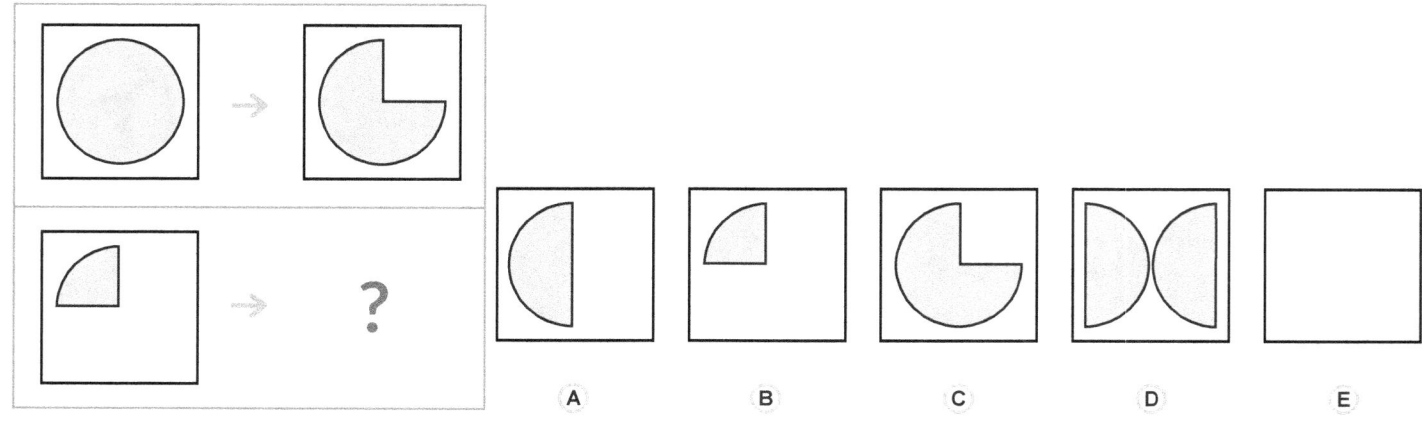

16

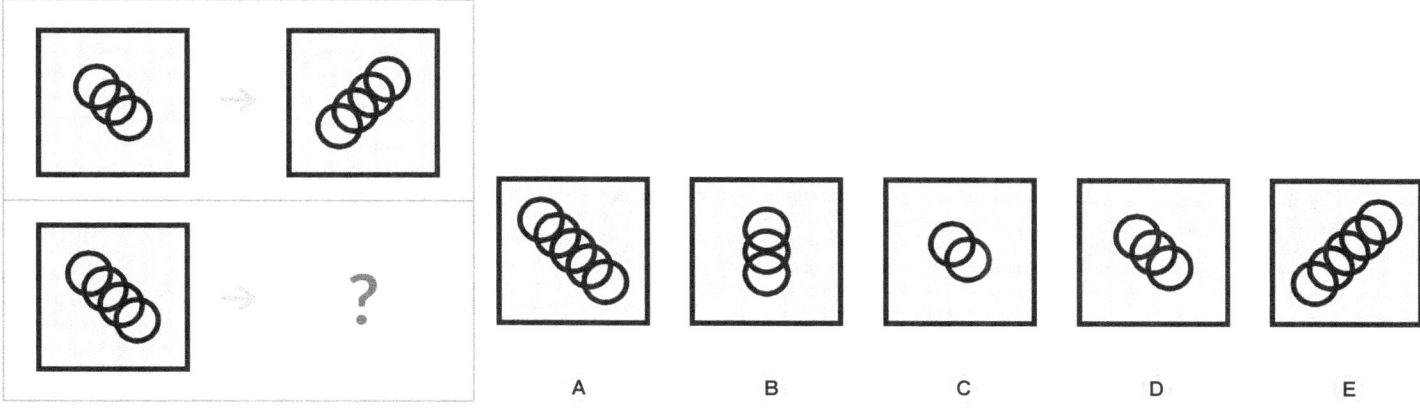

A   B   C   D   E

17

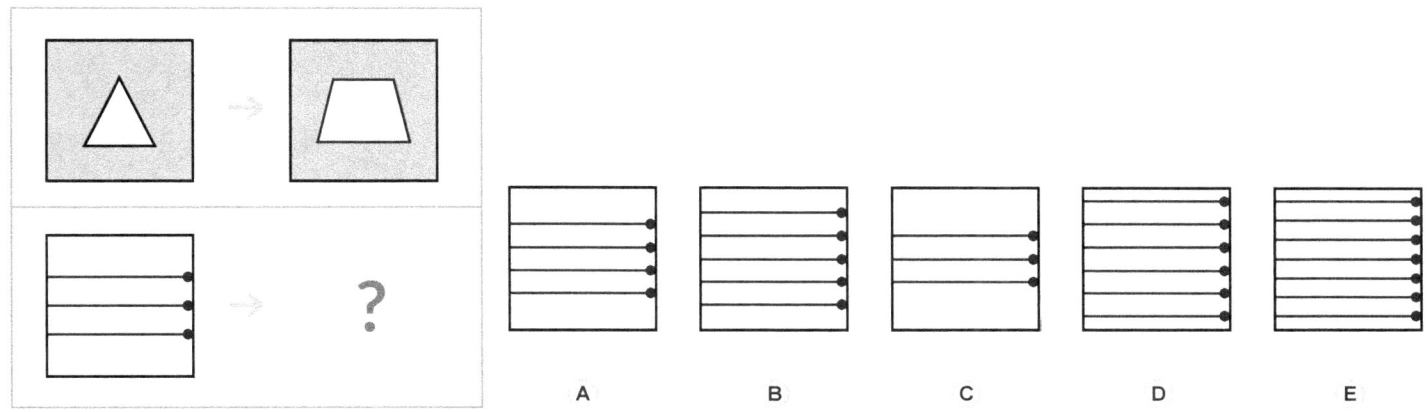

A   B   C   D   E

18

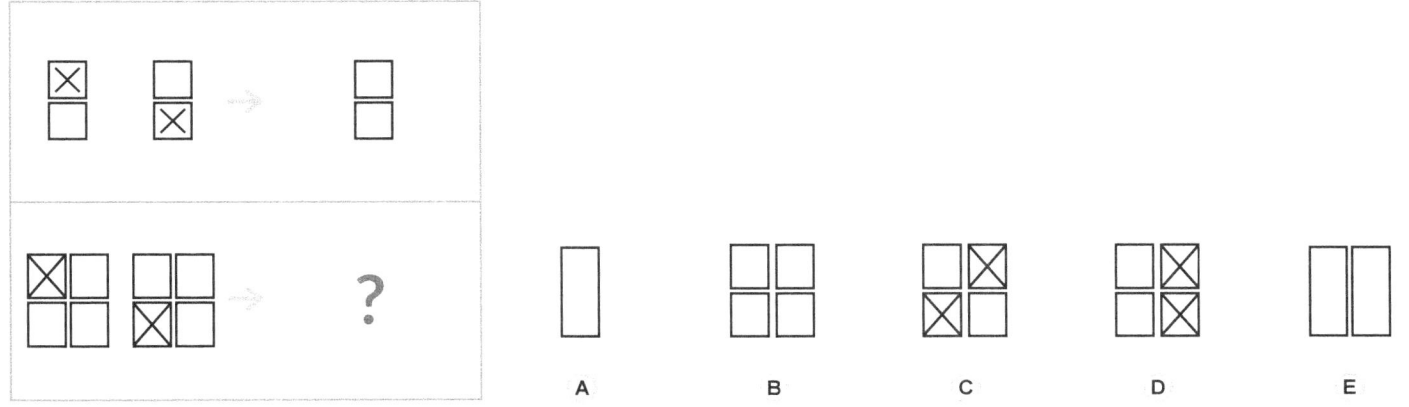

A   B   C   D   E

19

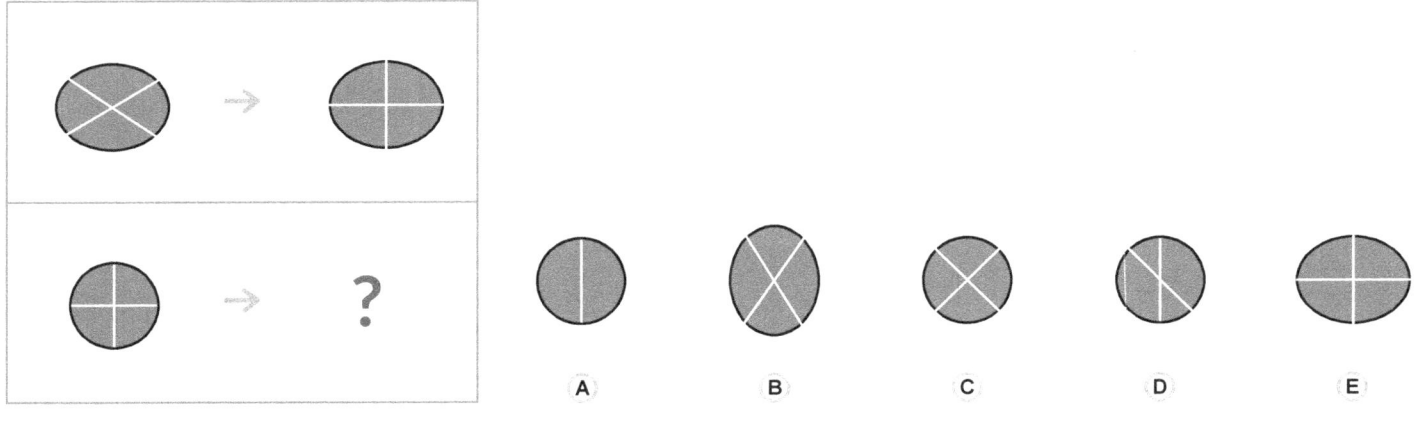

20

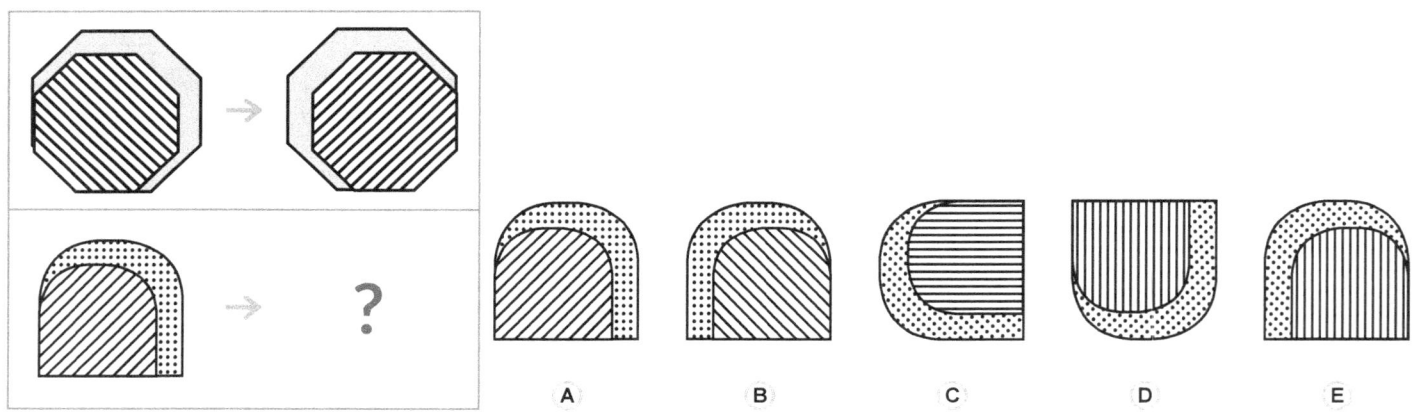

FIGURE CLASSIFICATION

Directions: The top row shows three pictures that are alike in some way. Look at the bottom row. Which bottom picture goes best with the top pictures?

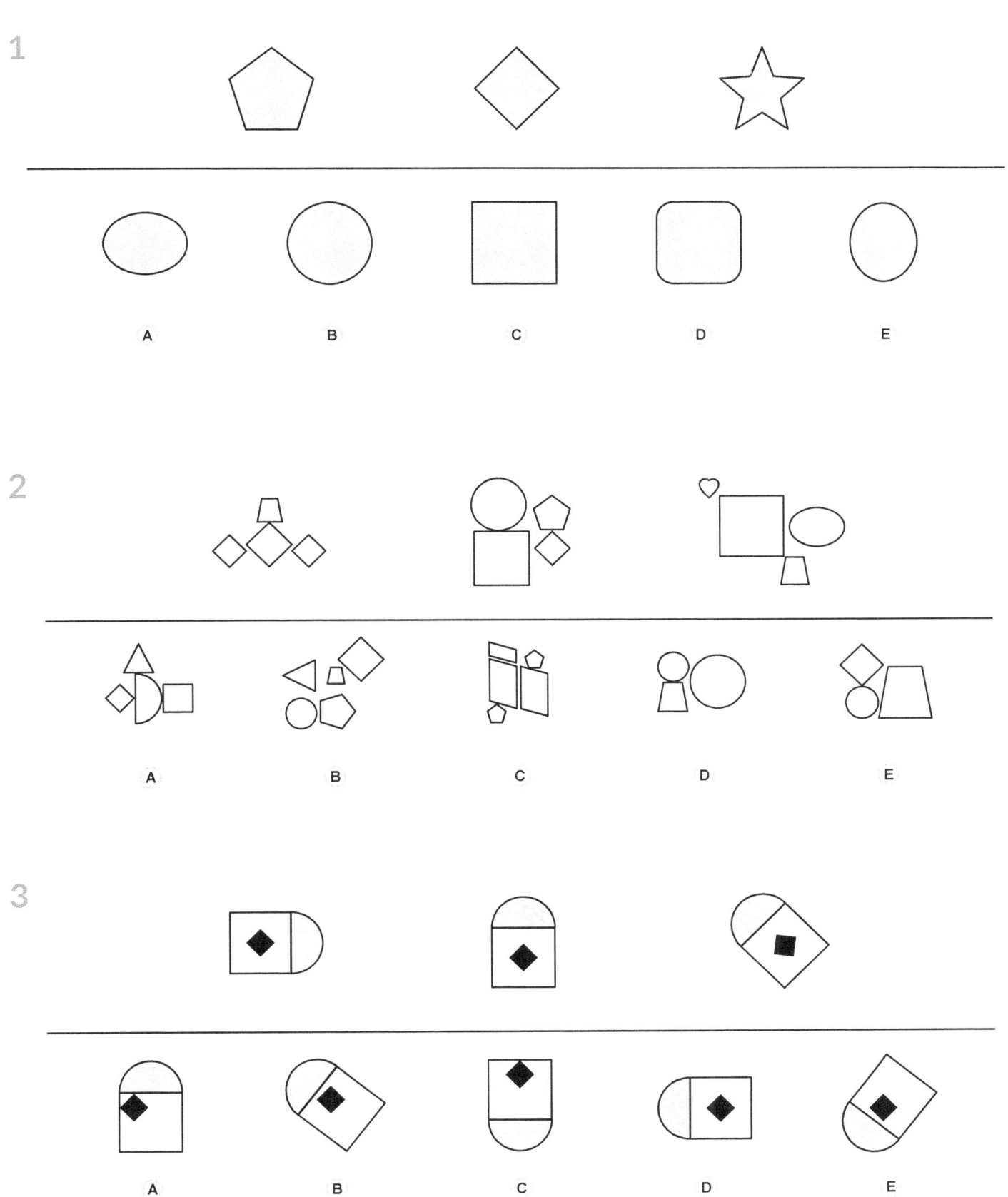

4

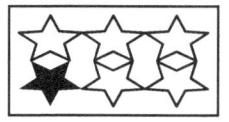 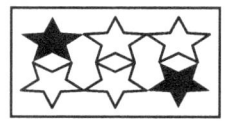   

Ⓐ   Ⓑ   Ⓒ   Ⓓ   Ⓔ

5

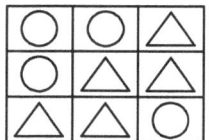 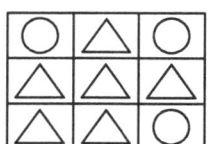 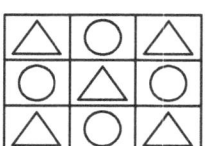

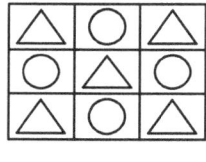 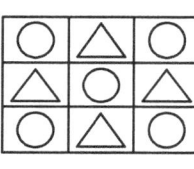 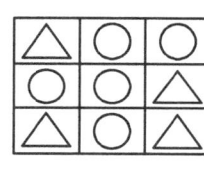

Ⓐ   Ⓑ   Ⓒ   Ⓓ

6

 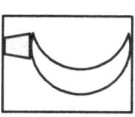 

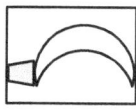  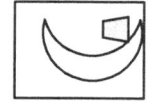  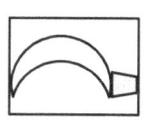

Ⓐ   Ⓑ   Ⓒ   Ⓓ   Ⓔ

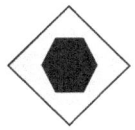 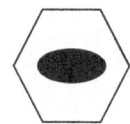 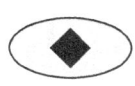

  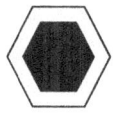 

A   B   C   D   E

8

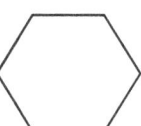  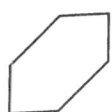

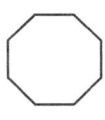  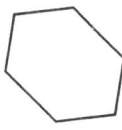 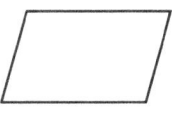

A   B   C   D   E

9

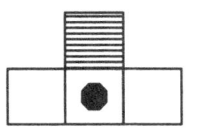 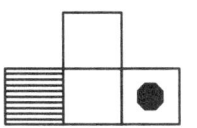 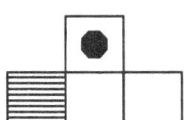

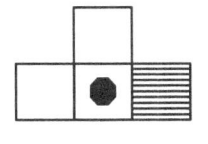 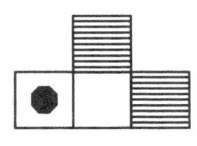 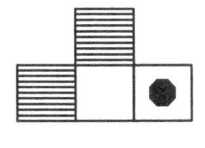 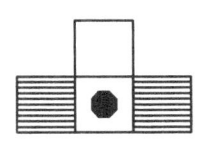 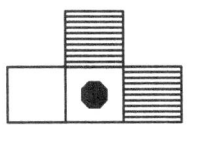

A   B   C   D   E

10

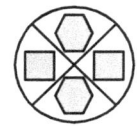  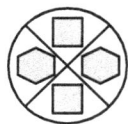

   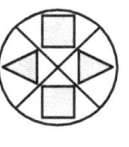

A   B   C   D   E

11

  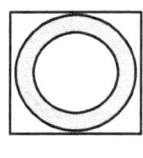 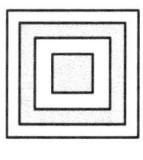 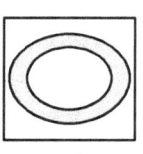

A   B   C   D   E

12

  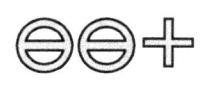 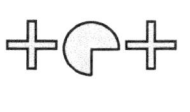 

A   B   C   D   E

13

A   B   C   D   E

14

▽ ▽ △ ▽   ▽ △ ▽ ▽   △ ▽ ▽ ▽

▽ ▽ ▽ △   ▽ △ △ △   △ △ ▽ ▽   △ ▽ △ ▽

A   B   C   D

15

   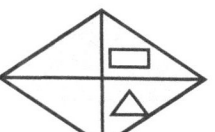

 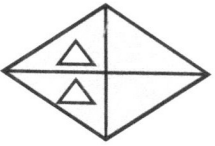 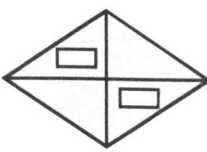 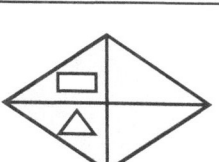

A   B   C   D

16

(A) (B) (C) (D) (E)

17

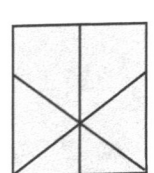 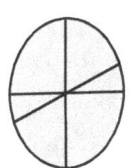 

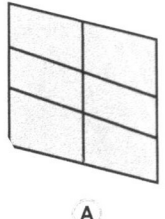 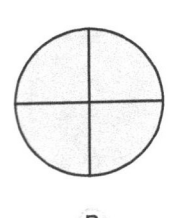 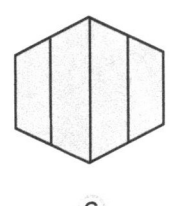 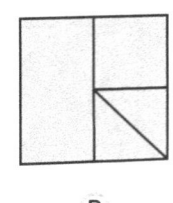 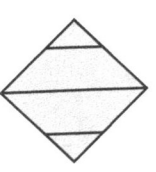

(A) (B) (C) (D) (E)

(C) (D) (E)

(E) 49

19

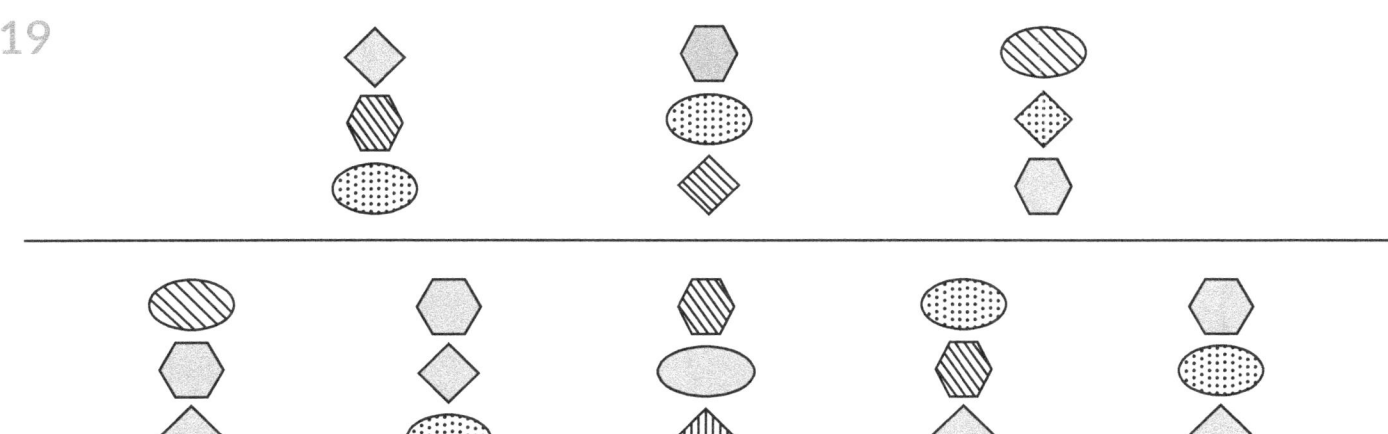

| A | B | C | D | E |

20

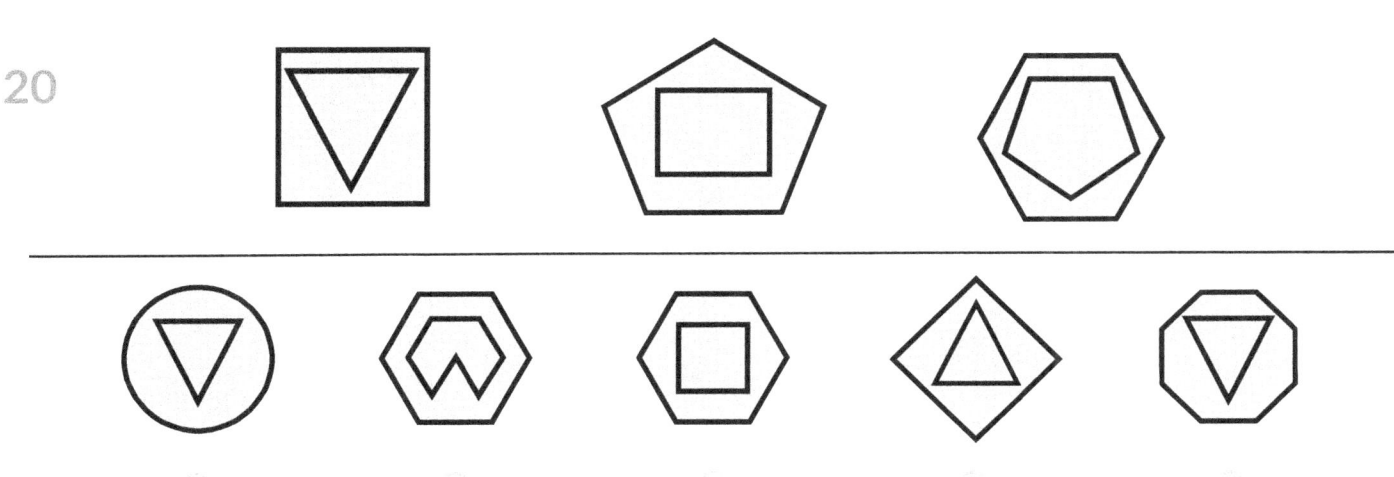

| A | B | C | D | E |

PAPER FOLDING

The top row of pictures shows a sheet of paper. The paper was folded, then something was cut out. Which picture in the bottom row shows how the paper would look after it's unfolded?

1.

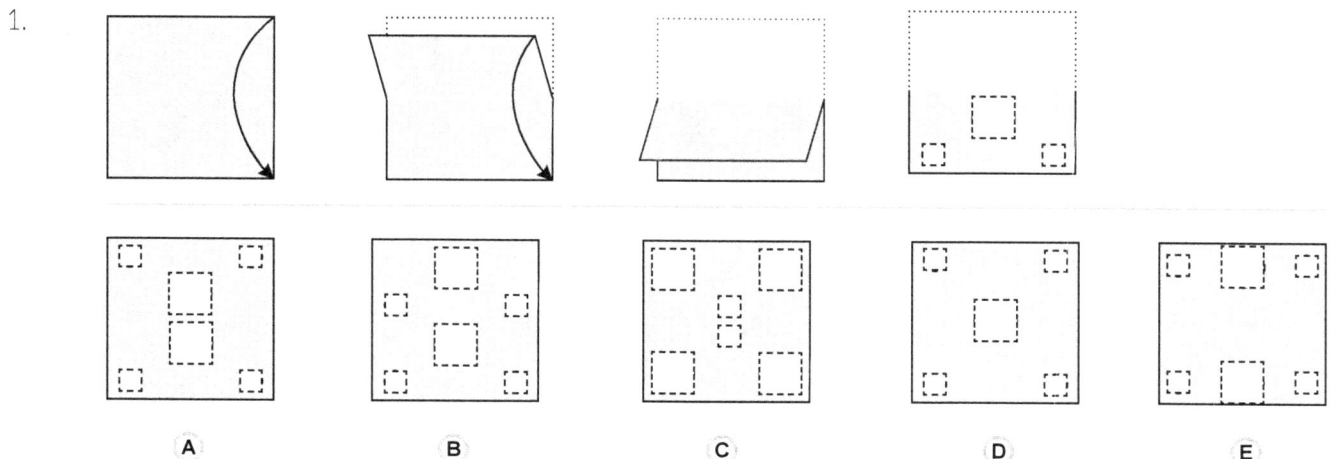

A   B   C   D   E

2.

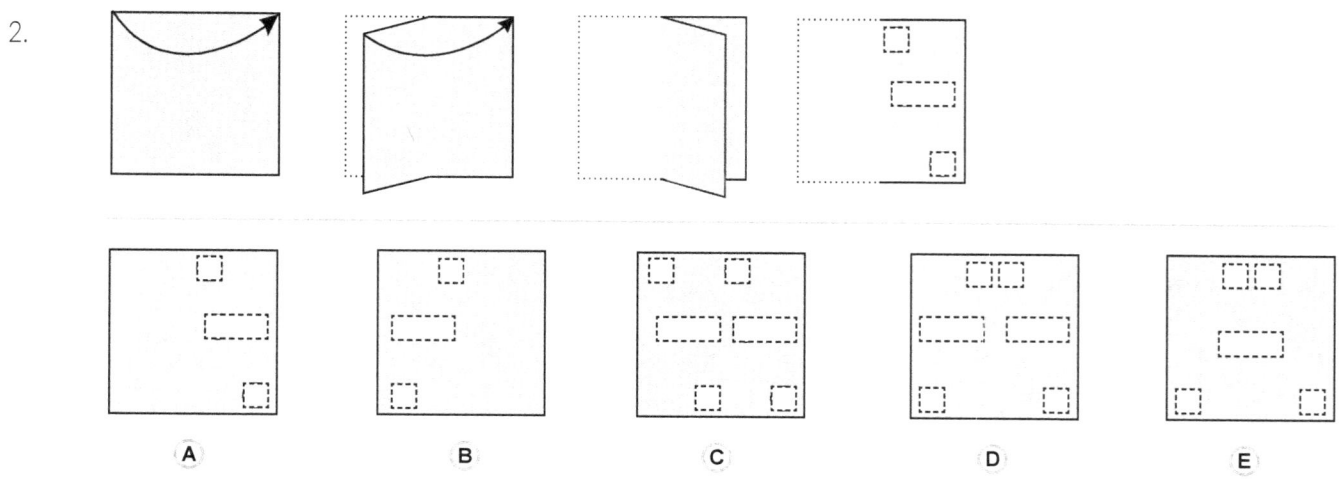

A   B   C   D   E

3.

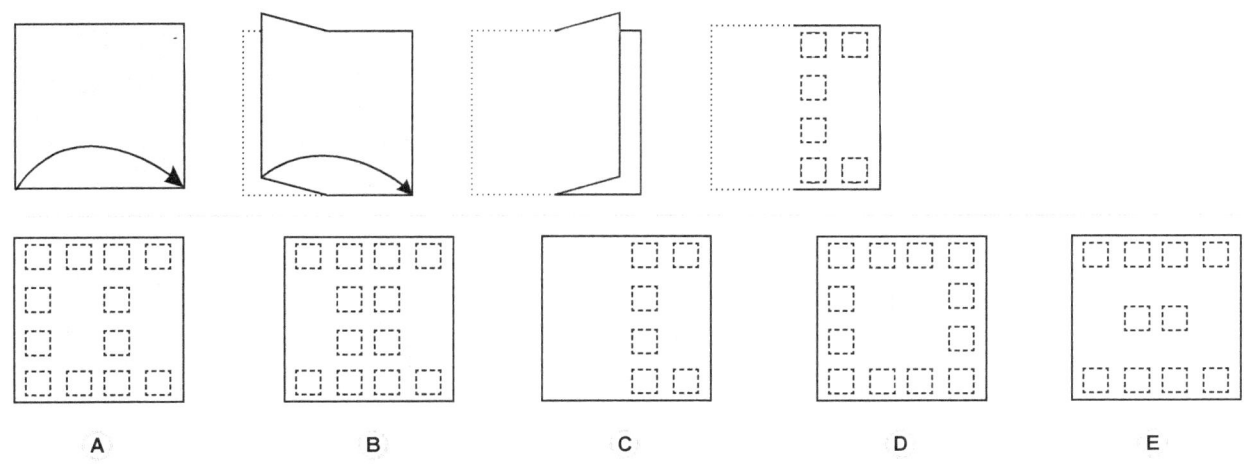

| A | B | C | D | E |

4.

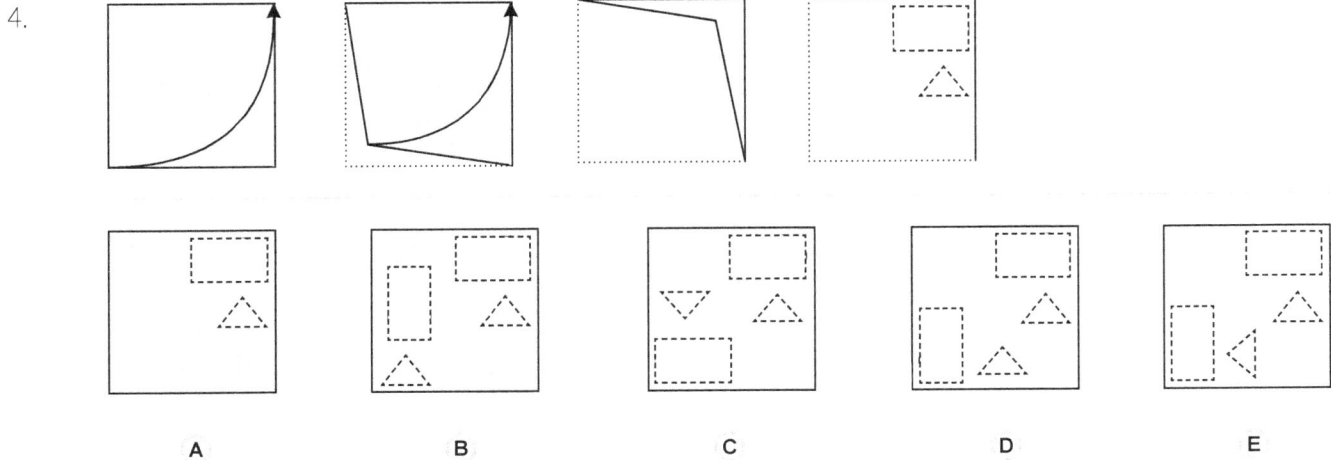

| A | B | C | D | E |

5.

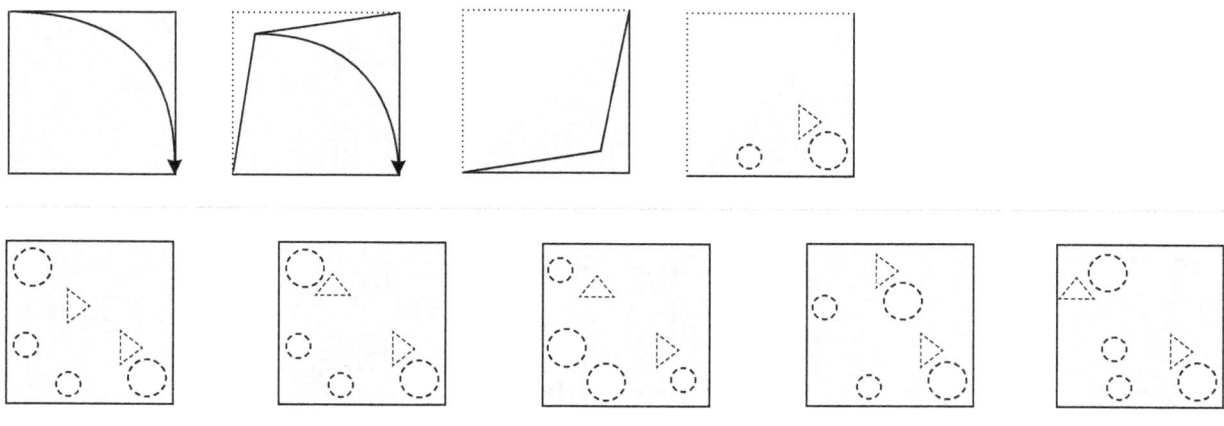

6.

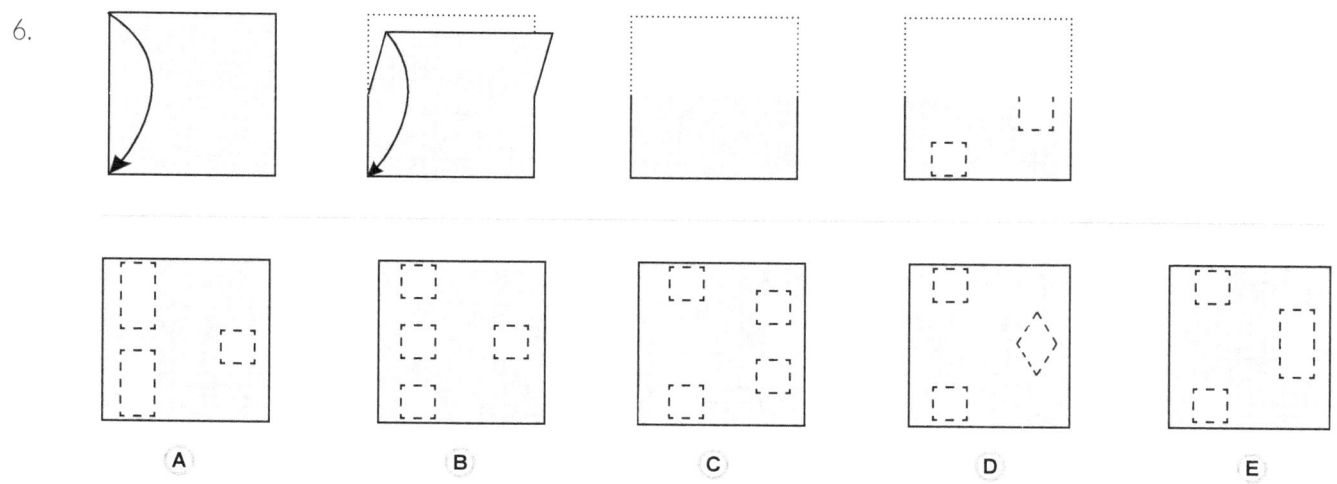

7.

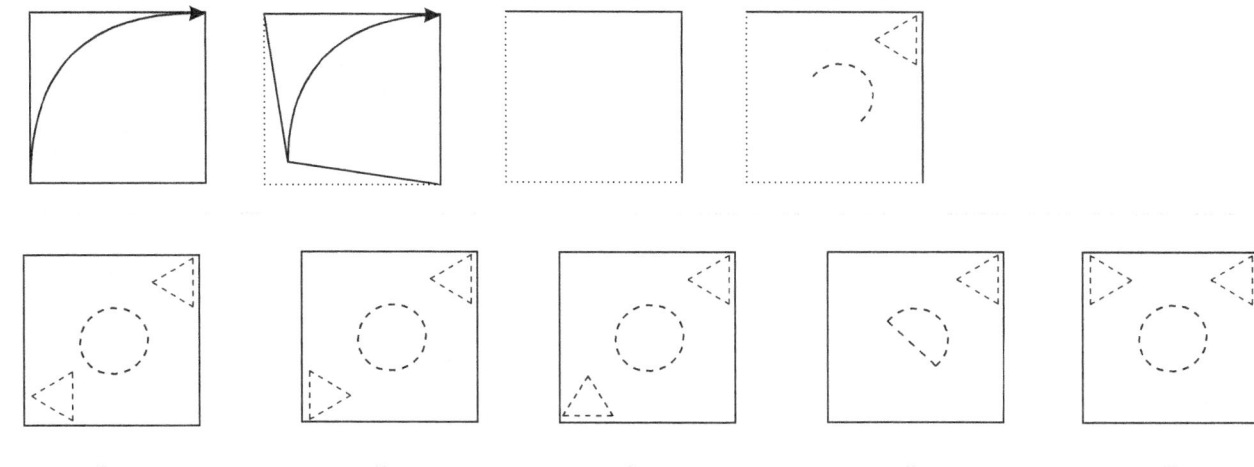

A   B   C   D   E

8.

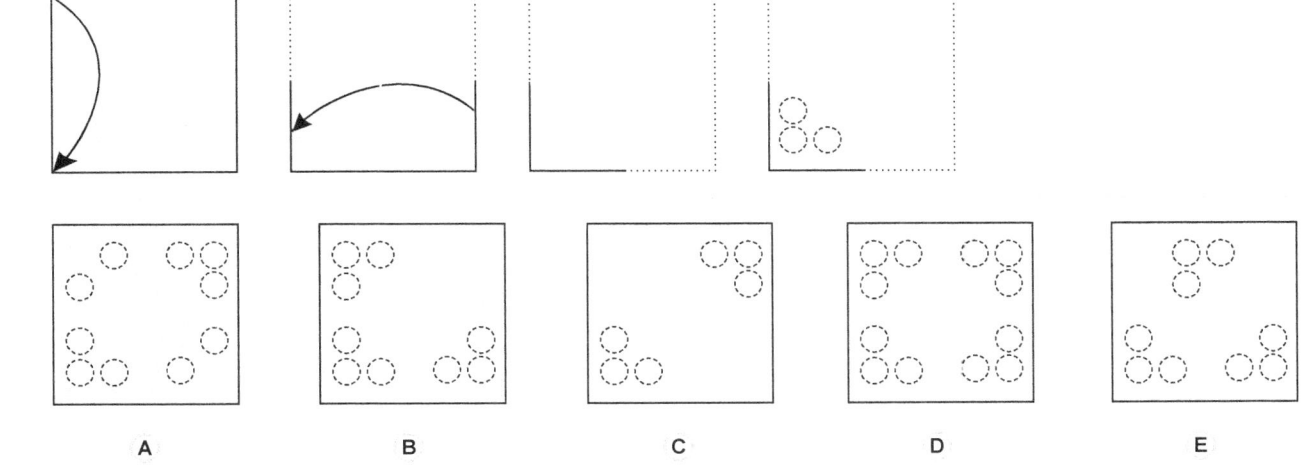

A   B   C   D   E

9.

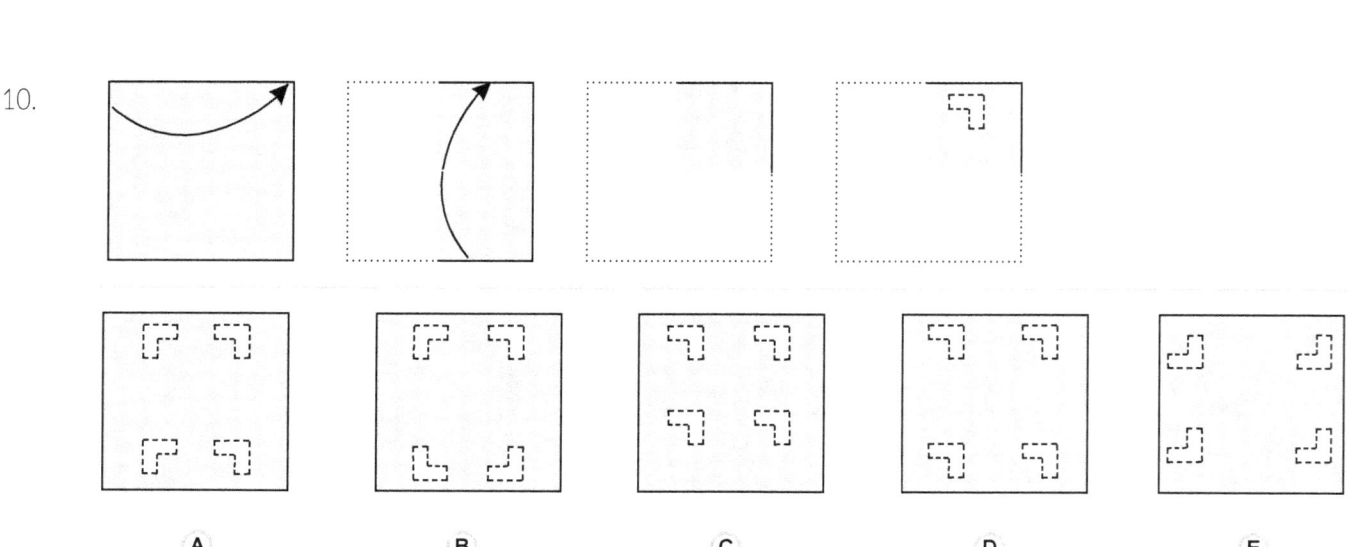

10.

11.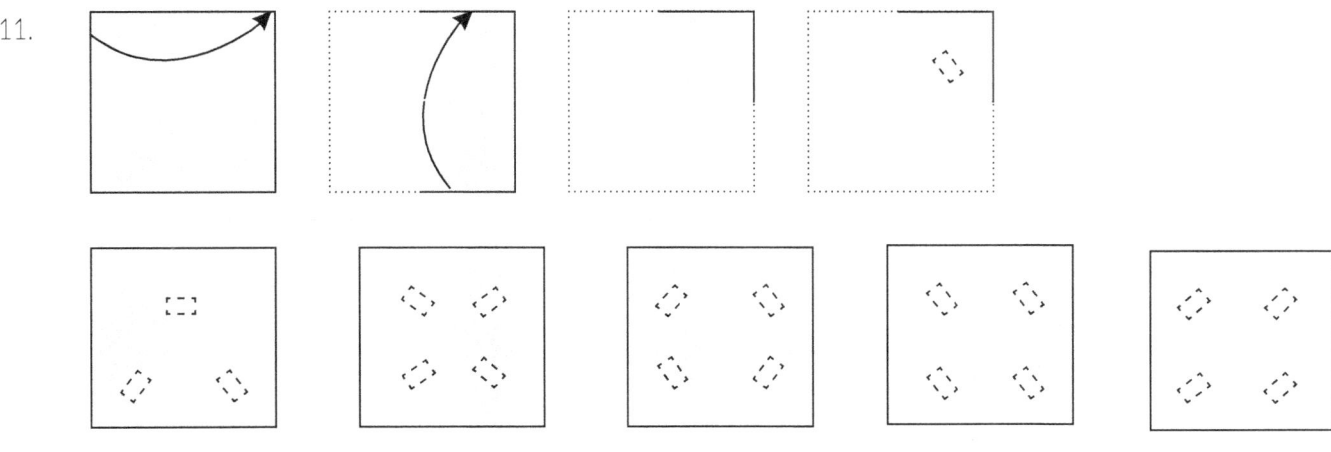

12.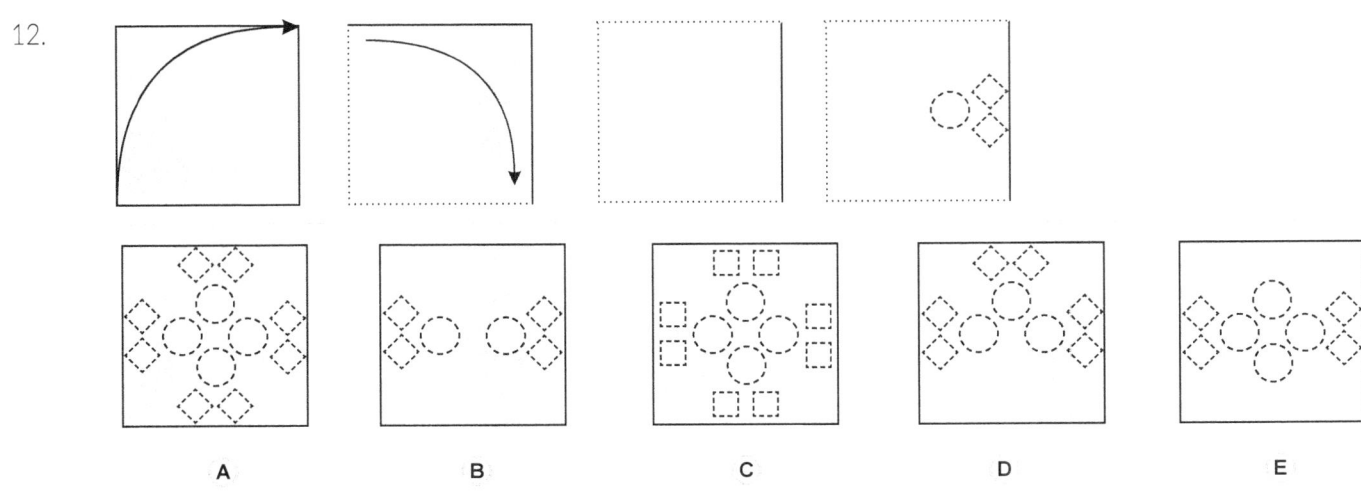

13.

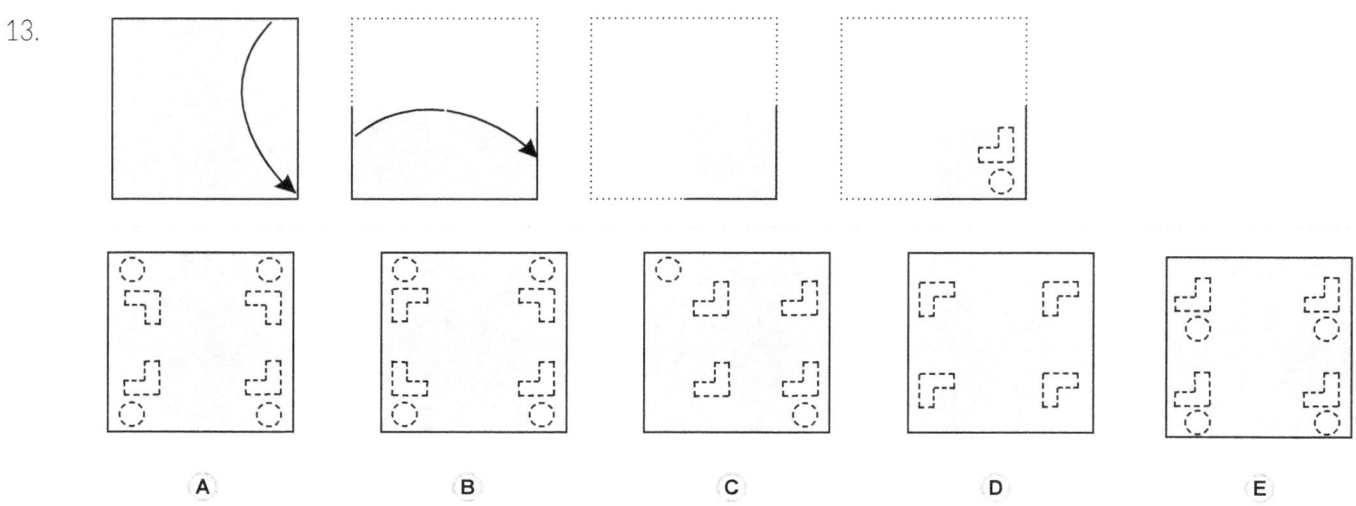

14.

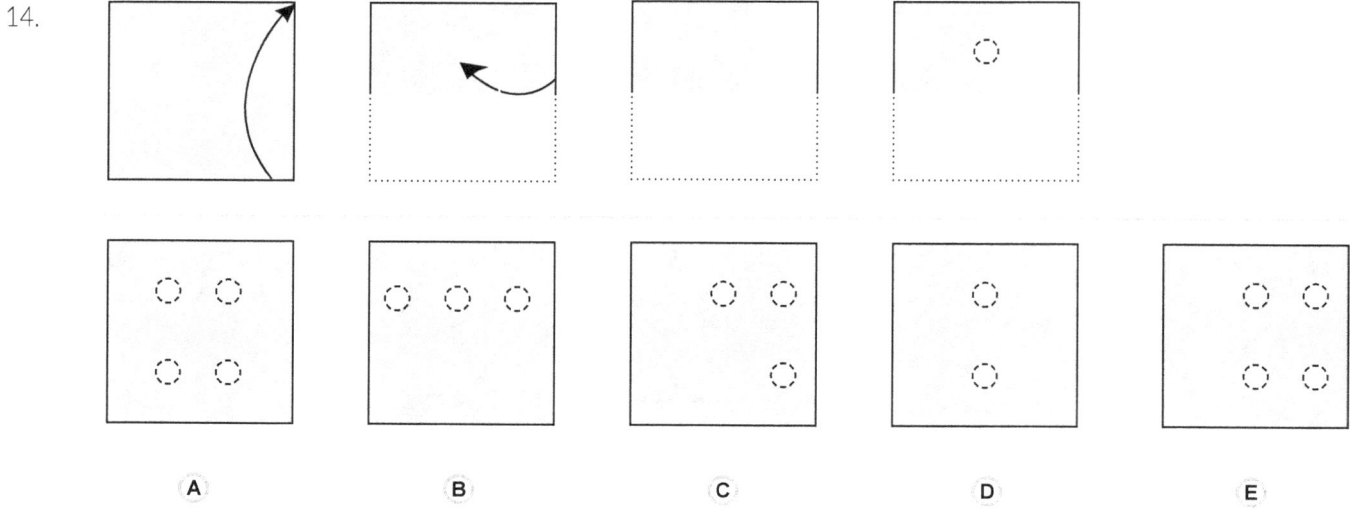

Caleb

- End of Practice Test 2 -
- Practice Test 3 begins on the next page. -

Directions: The pictures in the top boxes go together in some way. One of the bottom boxes is empty. Which answer choice goes with the picture in the bottom box in the same way the top pictures do?

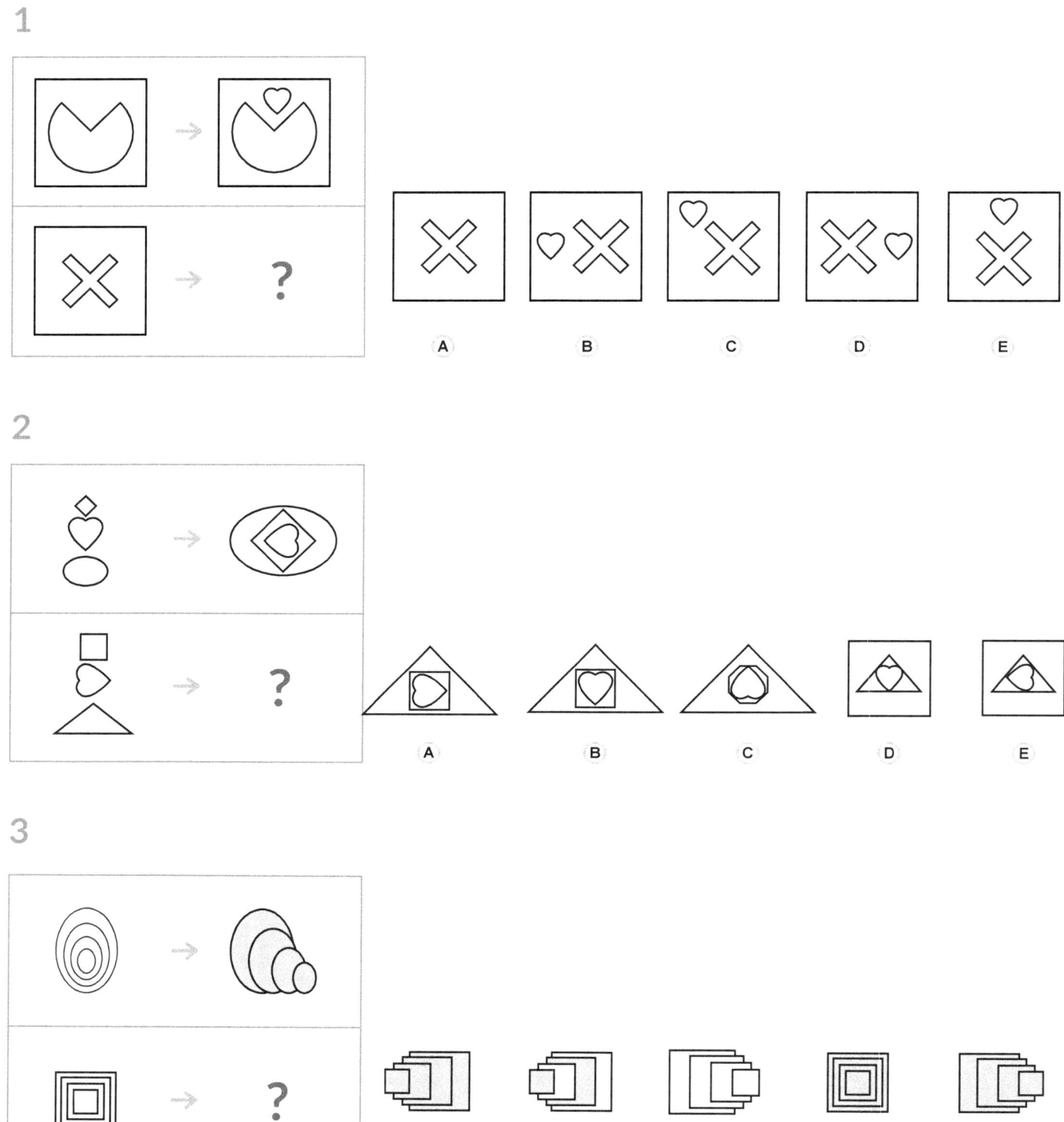

1

2

3

4

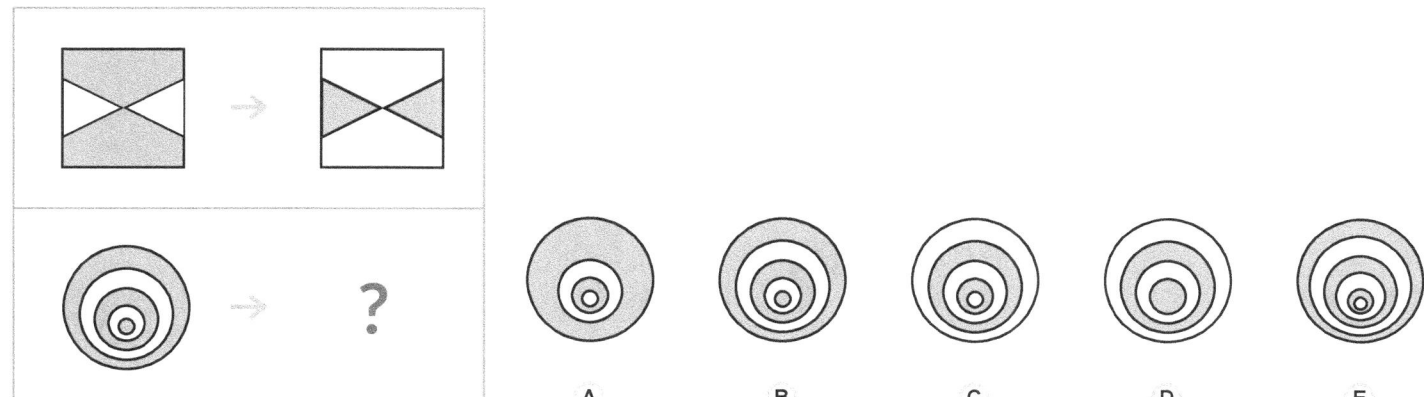

A   B   C   D   E

5

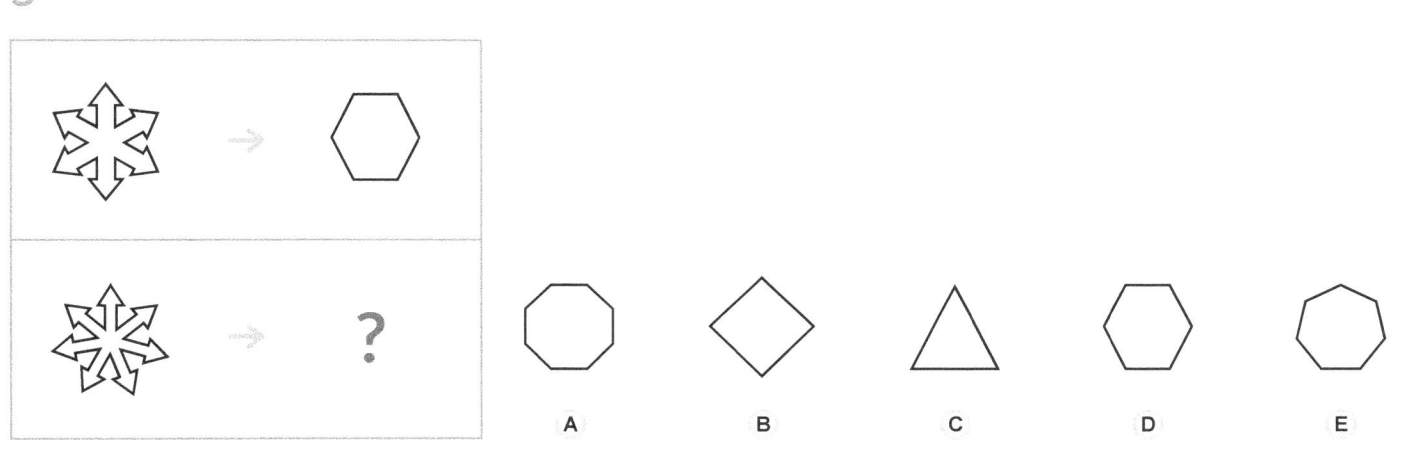

A   B   C   D   E

6

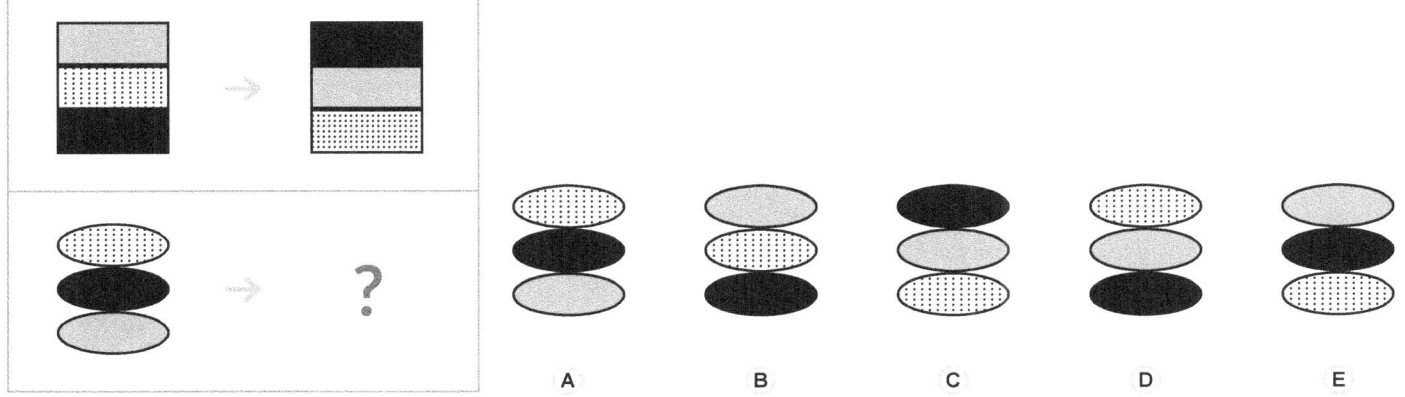

A   B   C   D   E

7

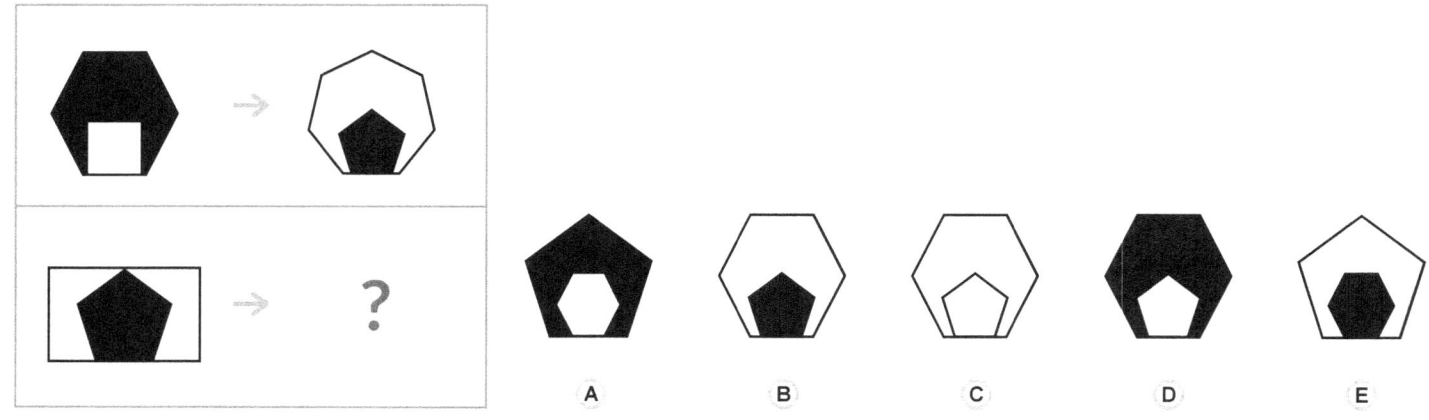

8

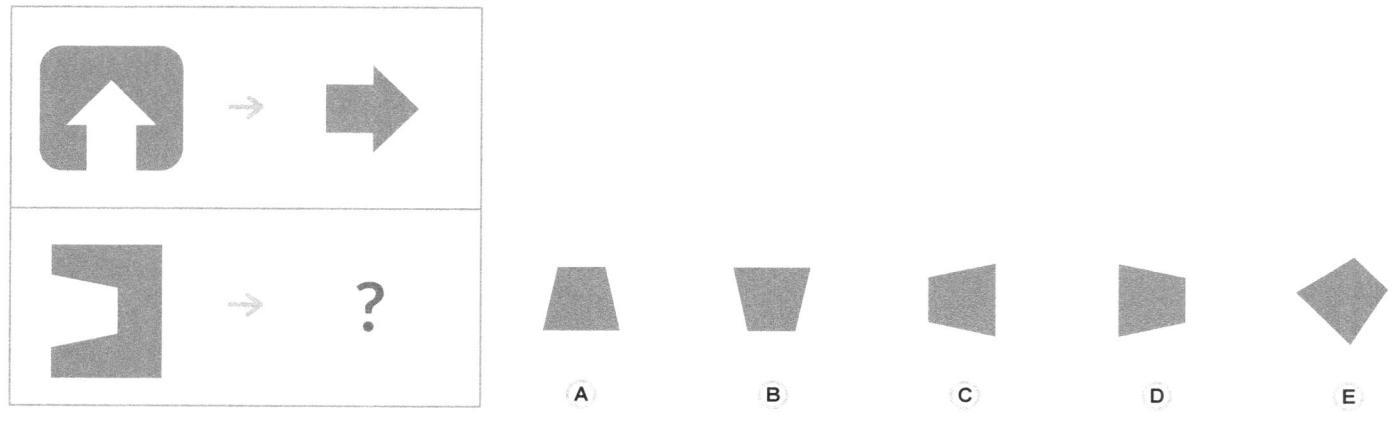

9

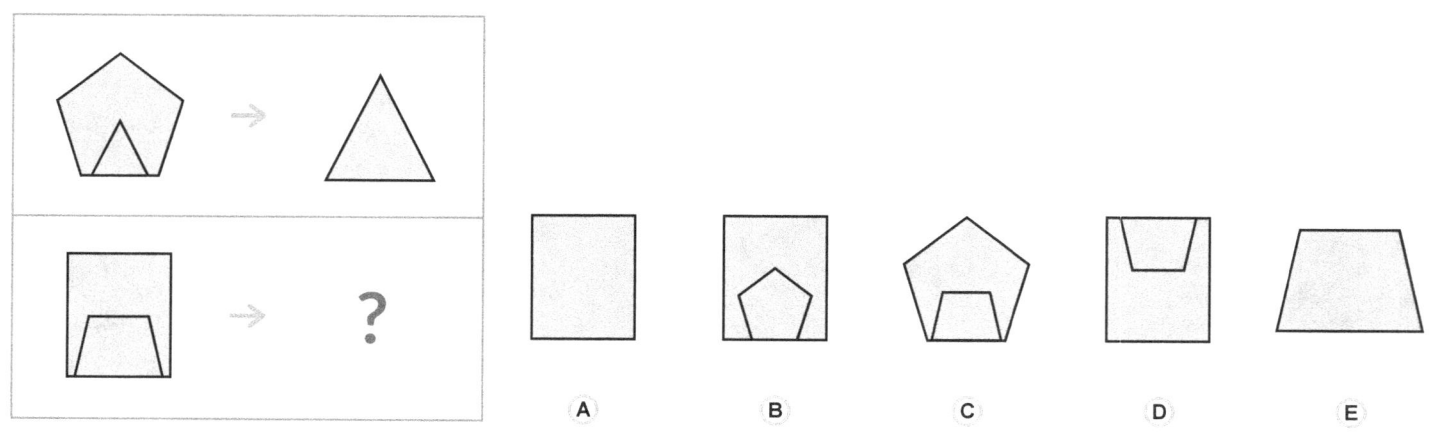

10

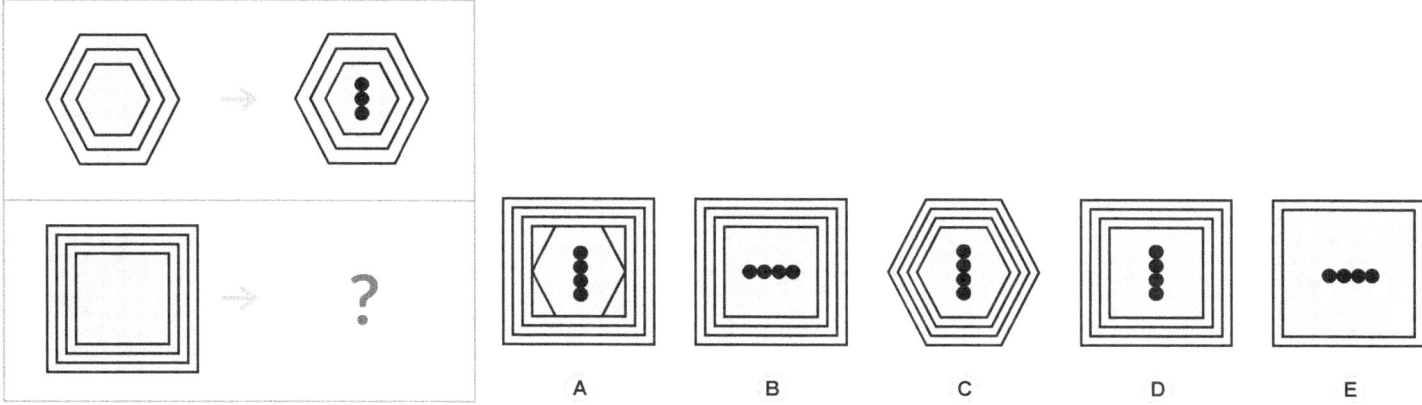

A B C D E

11

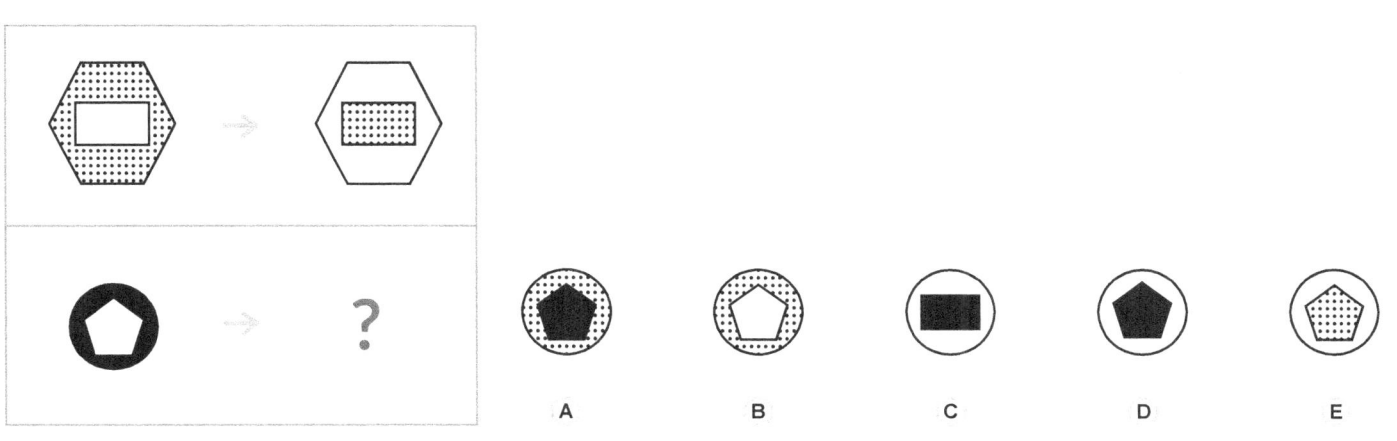

A B C D E

12

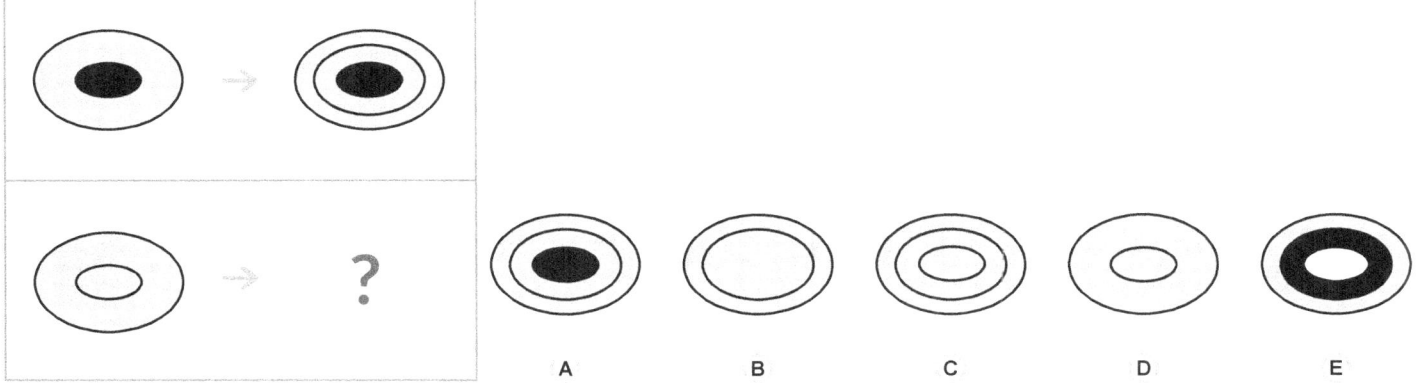

A B C D E

13

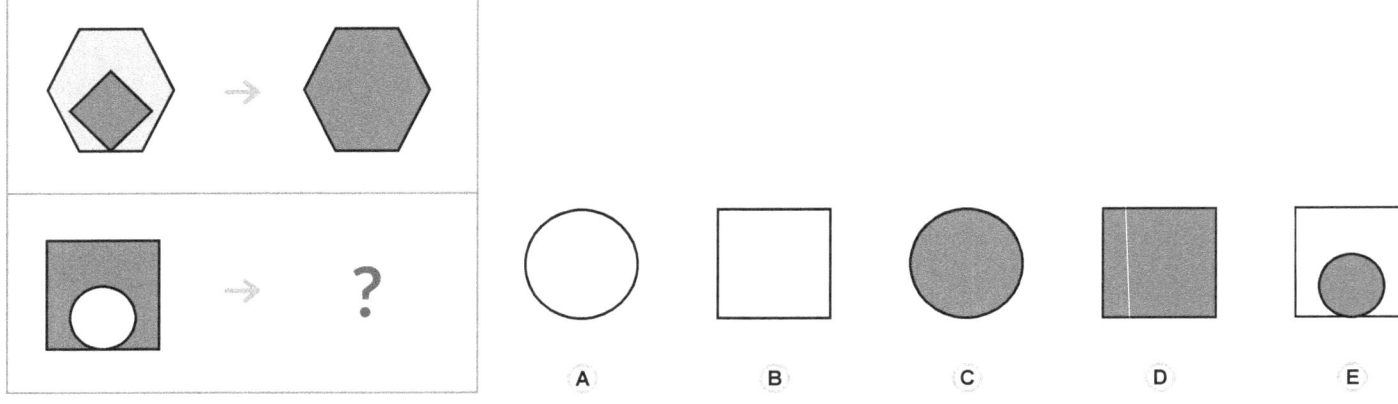

14

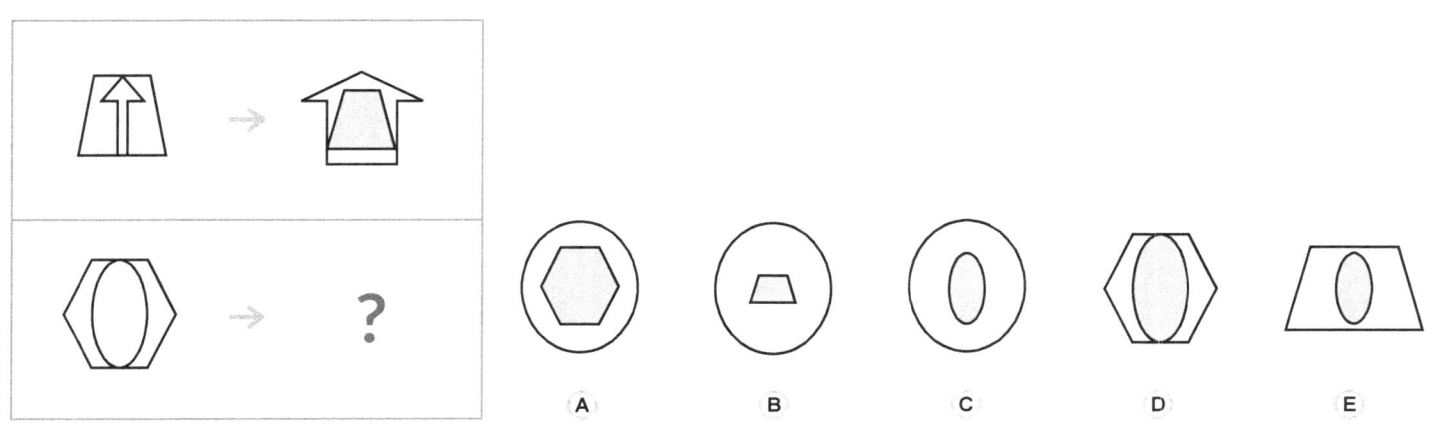

15

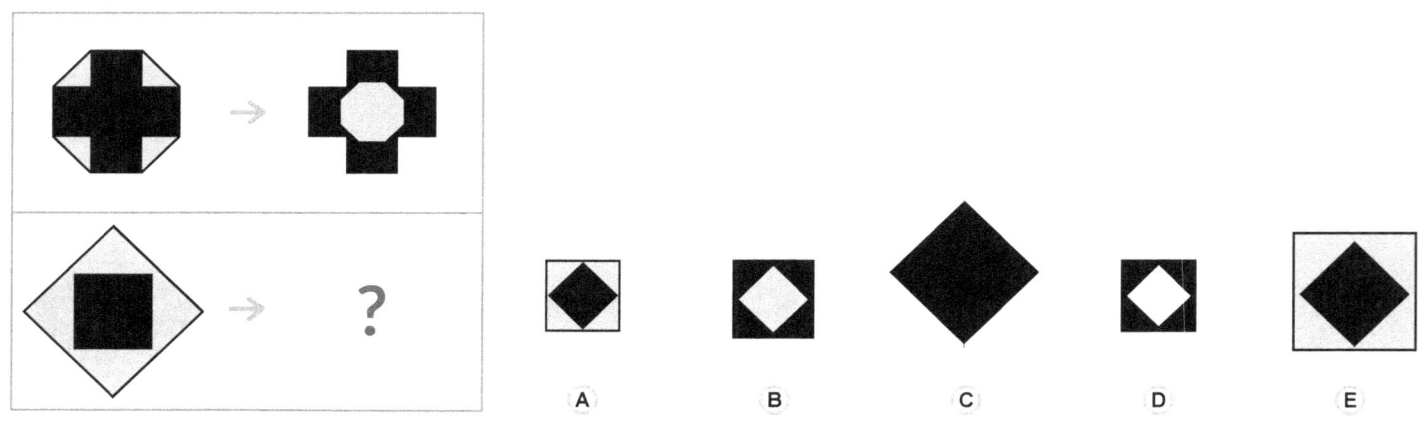

16

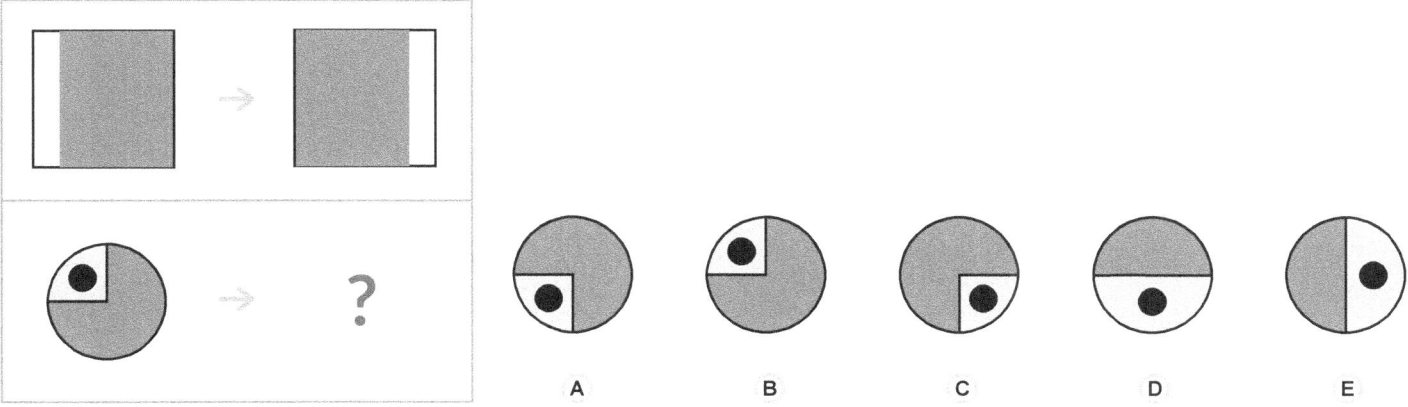

17

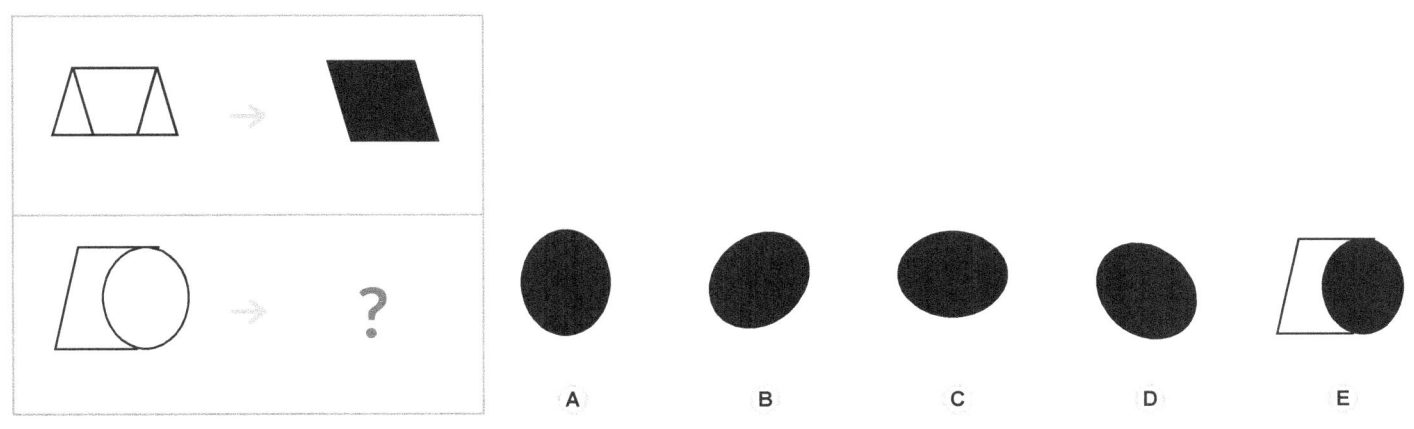

18

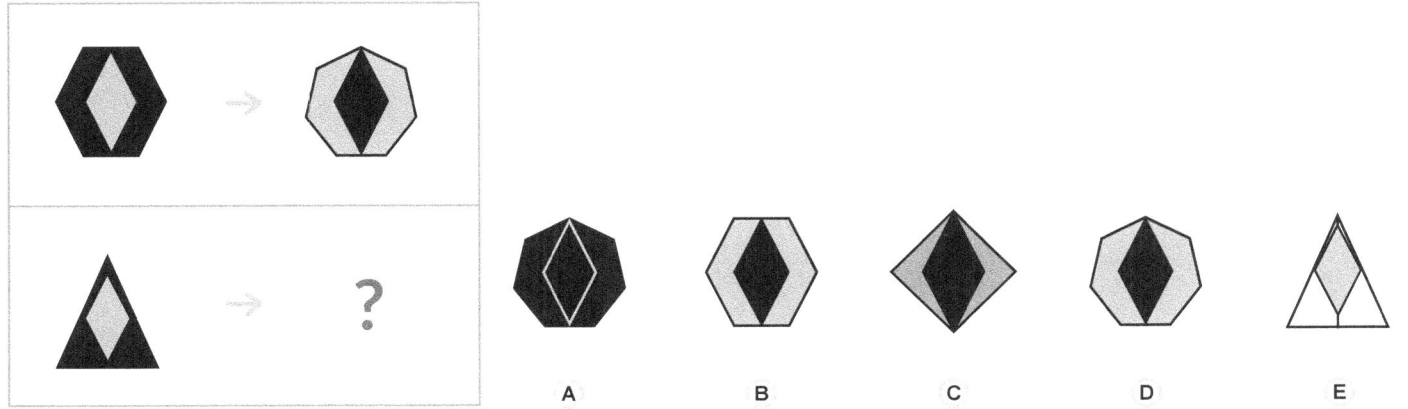

19

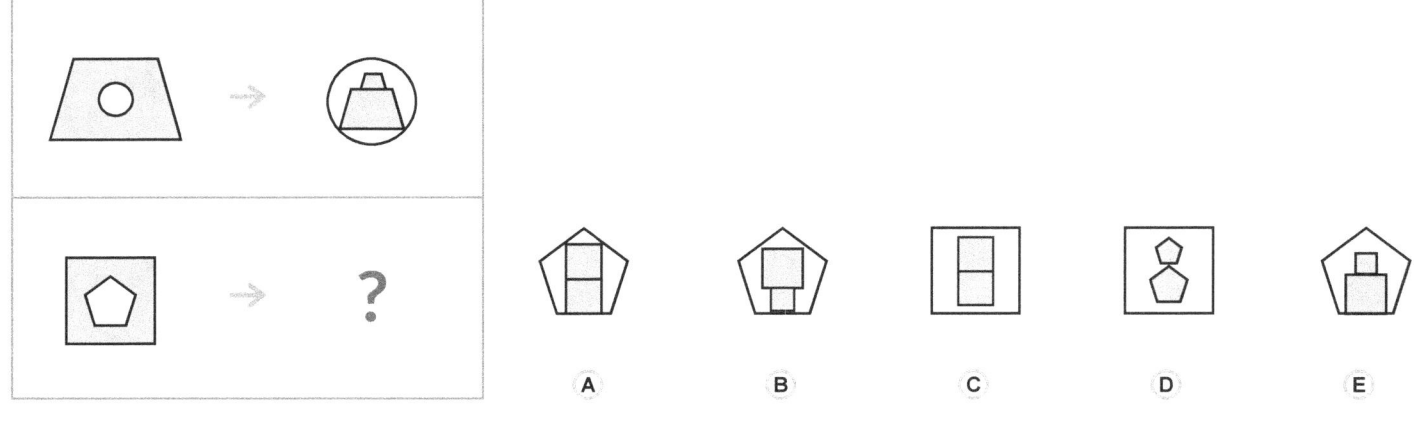

20

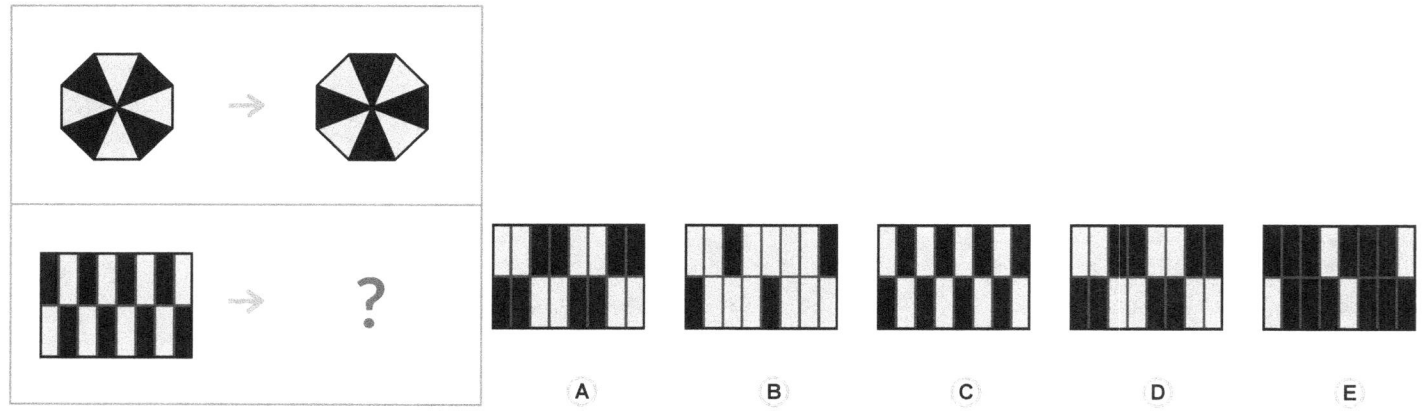

FIGURE CLASSIFICATION

Directions: The top row shows three pictures that are alike in some way. Look at the bottom row. Which bottom picture goes best with the top pictures?

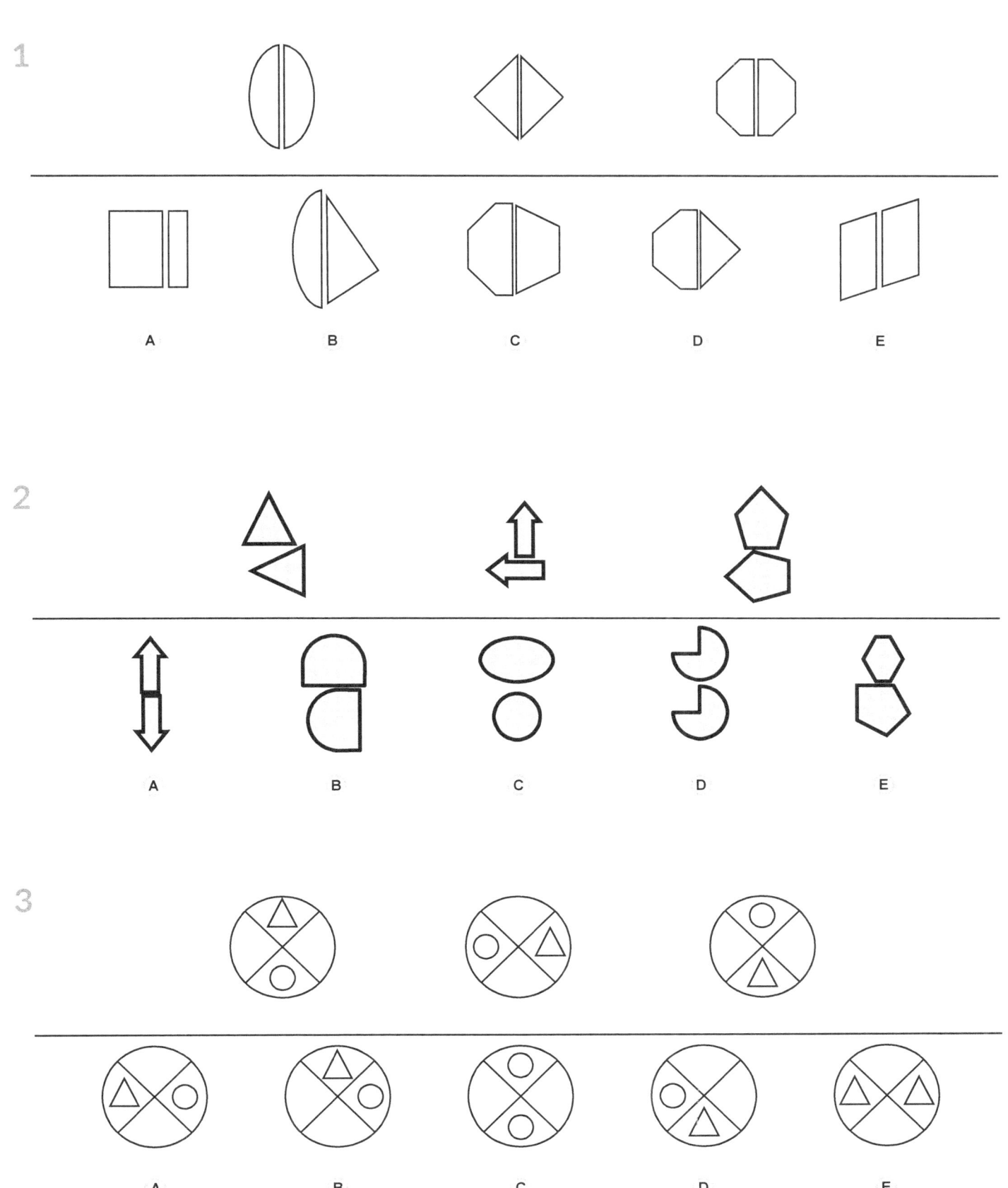

4

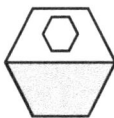 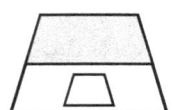 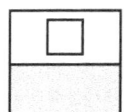

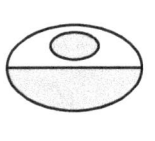  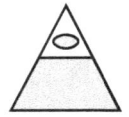 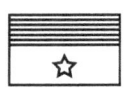 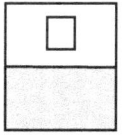

Ⓐ   Ⓑ   Ⓒ   Ⓓ   Ⓔ

5

  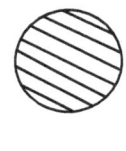 

Ⓐ   Ⓑ   Ⓒ   Ⓓ   Ⓔ

6

   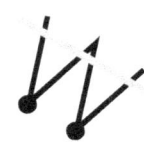 

Ⓐ   Ⓑ   Ⓒ   Ⓓ   Ⓔ

7

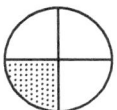 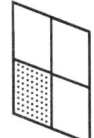 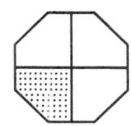

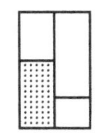  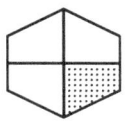 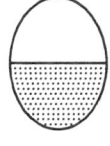 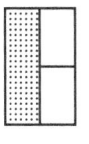

A   B   C   D   E

8

 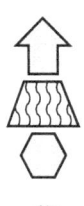  

A   B   C   D   E

9

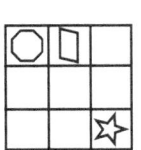 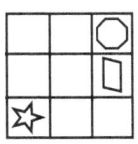 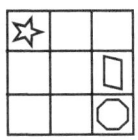

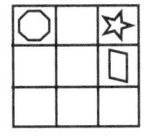 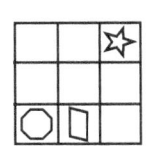 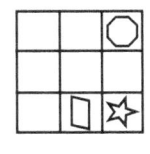 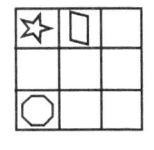 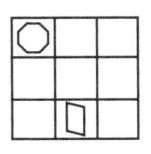

A   B   C   D   E

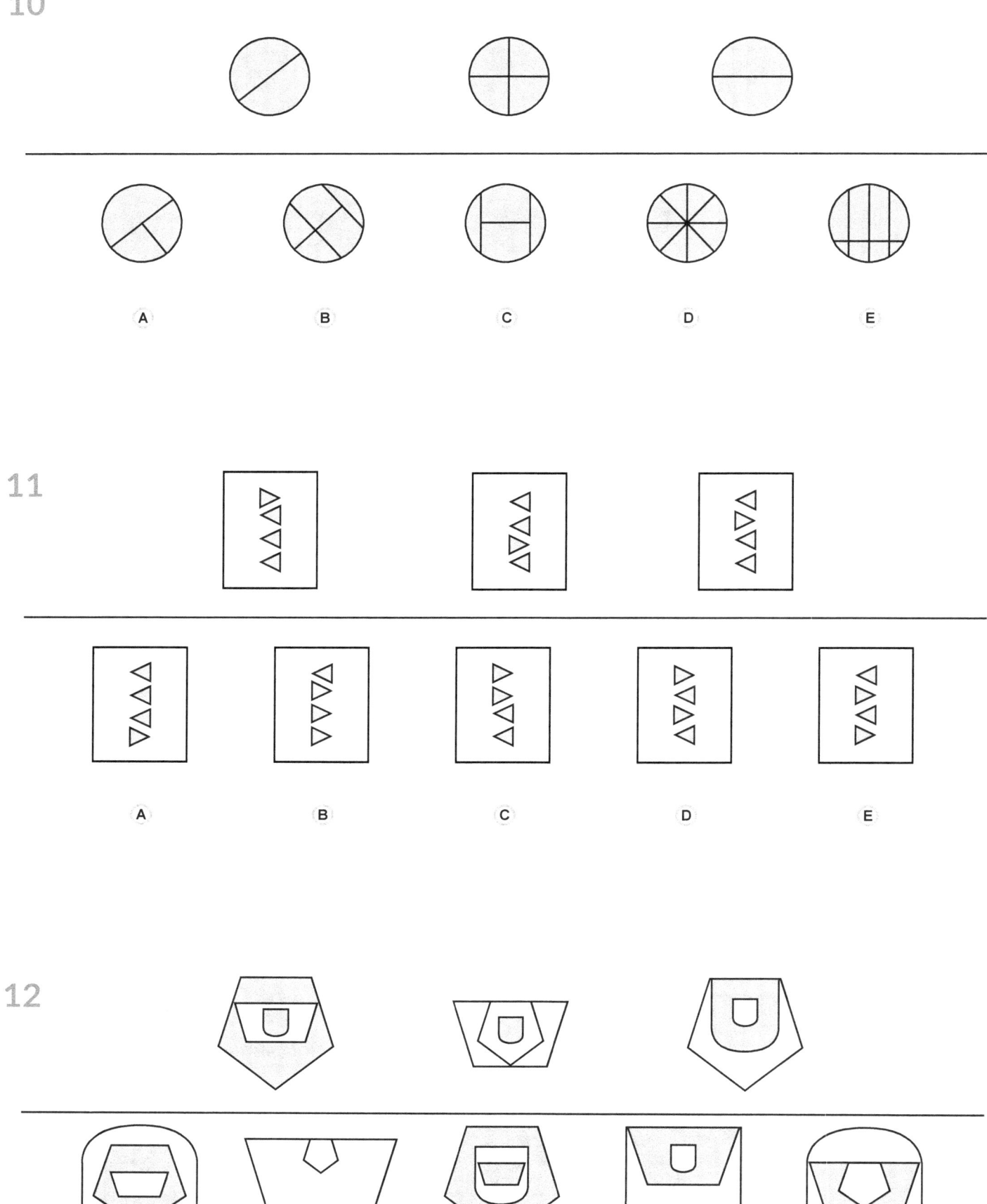

10

11

12

13

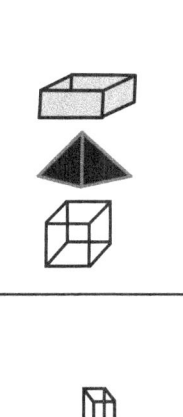 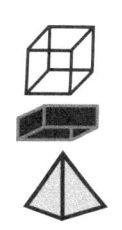 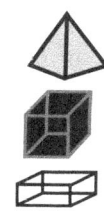

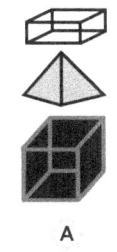 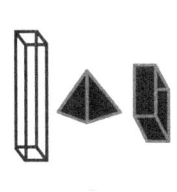 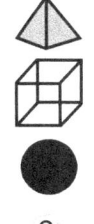  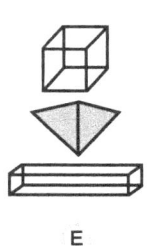

A   B   C   D   E

14

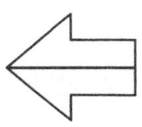  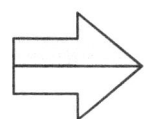

   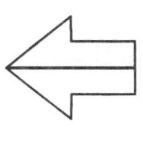 

A   B   C   D   E

15

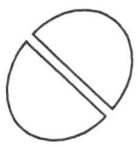 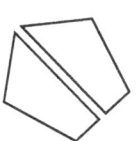 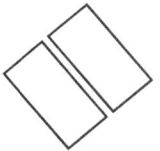

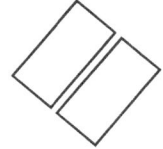 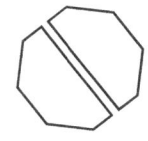 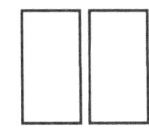 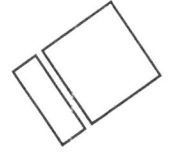 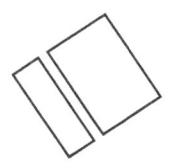

A   B   C   D   E

BTV   TVB   VBT

VⱢB   TBV   BVT   ΛTB   TBV

Ⓐ   Ⓑ   Ⓒ   Ⓓ   Ⓔ

17

Ⓐ   Ⓑ   Ⓒ   Ⓓ   Ⓔ

18

 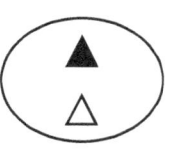   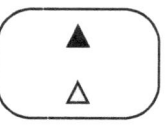

A   B   C   D   E

19

 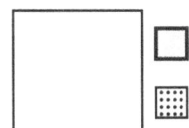 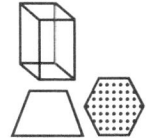

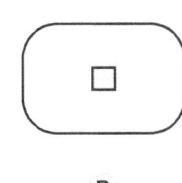   

A   B   C   D   E

20

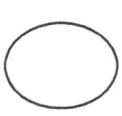  

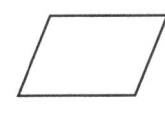 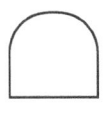 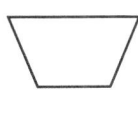 

A   B   C   D   E

PAPER FOLDING

Which picture in the bottom row shows how the paper would look after it's unfolded?

1.

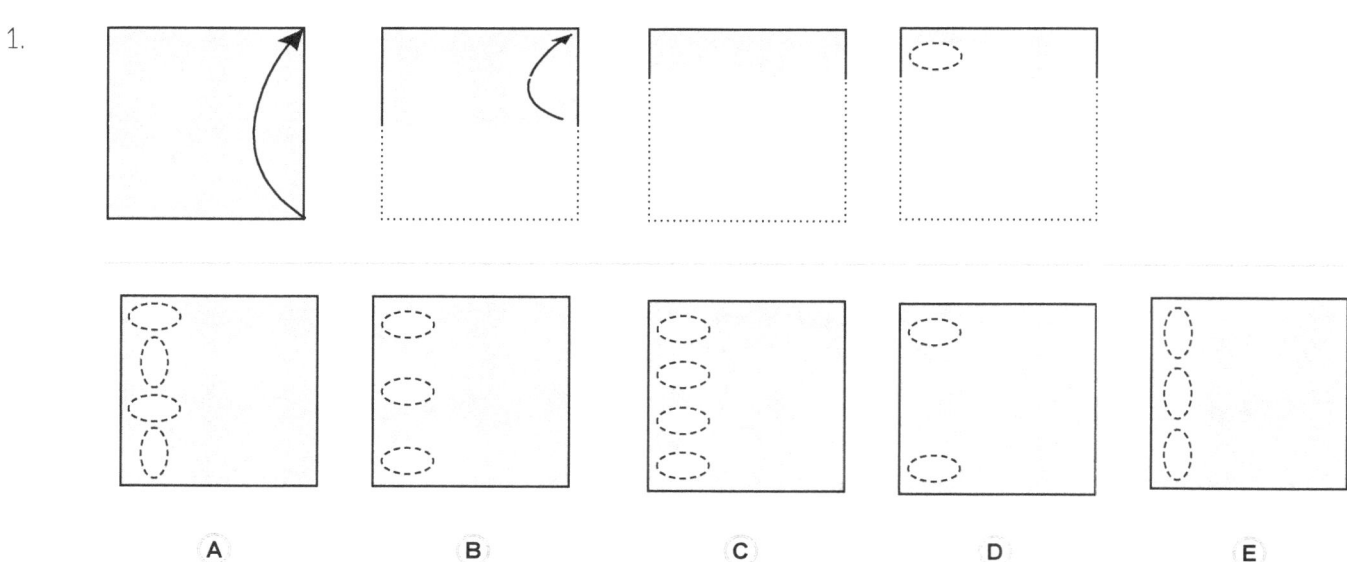

2.

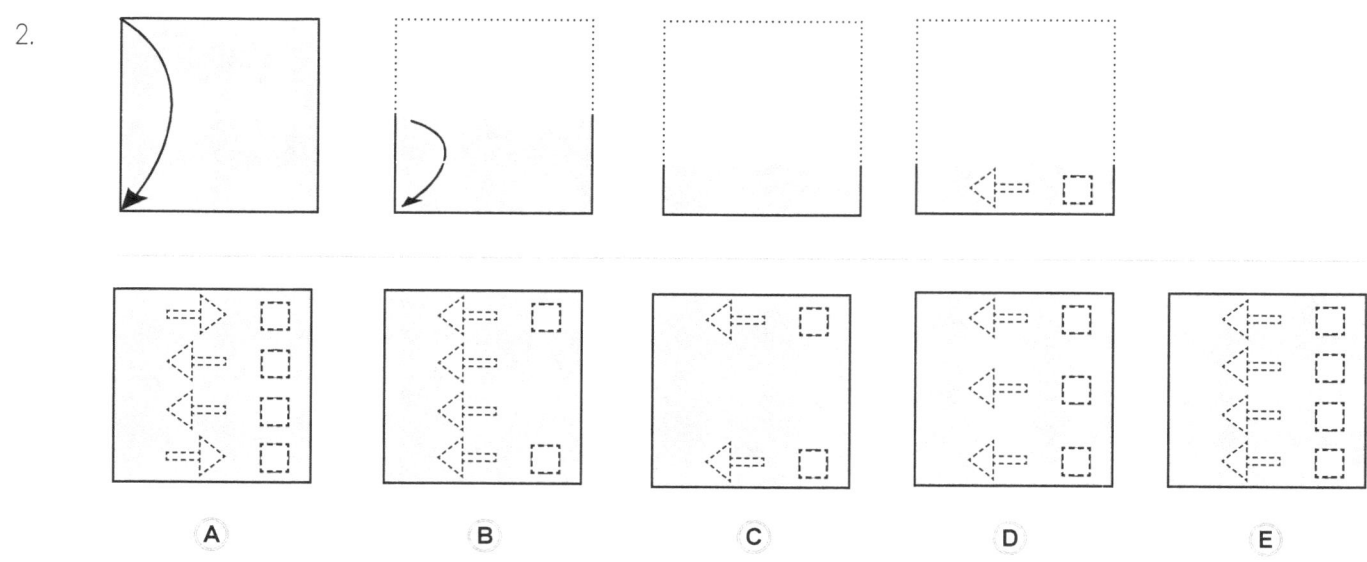

3.

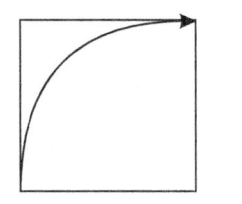 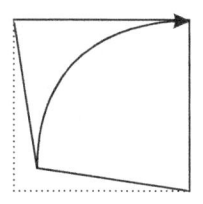  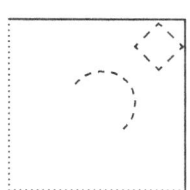

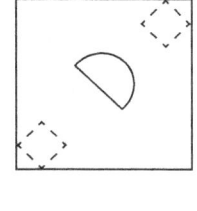 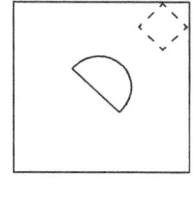 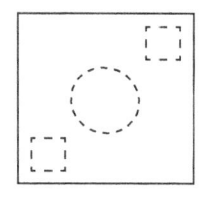 

   A   B   C   D   E

4.

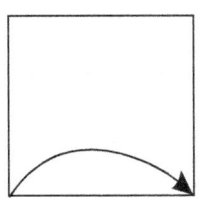 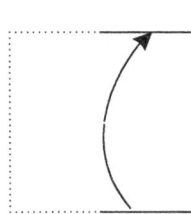  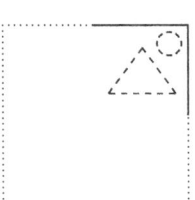

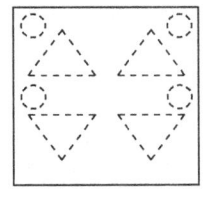 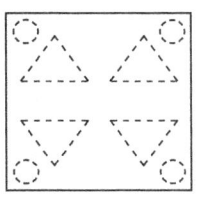 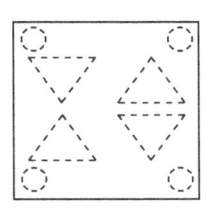 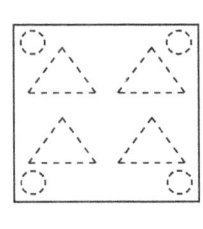 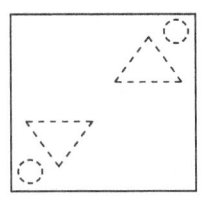

   A   B   C   D   E

5.

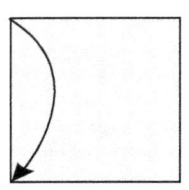 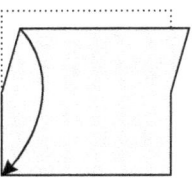 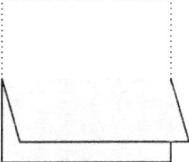 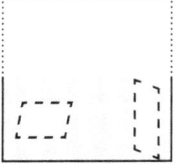

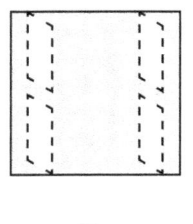 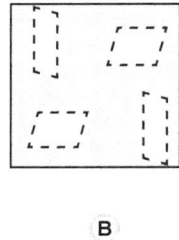 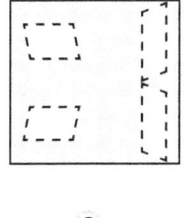 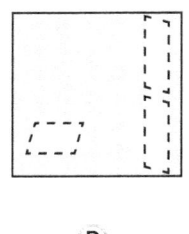 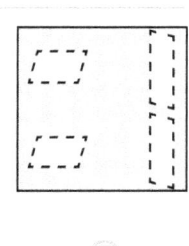

    A   B   C   D   E

6.

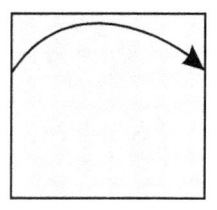 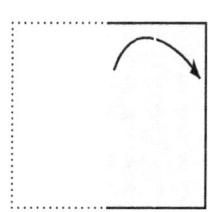  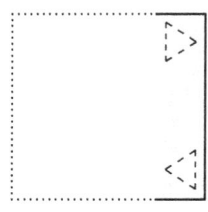

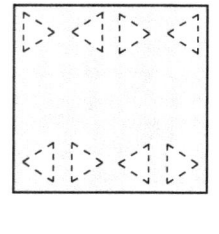 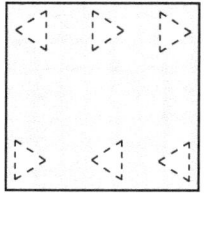 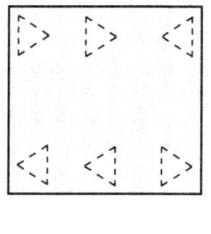 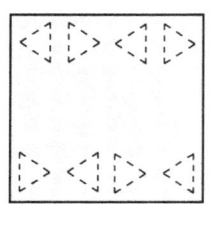 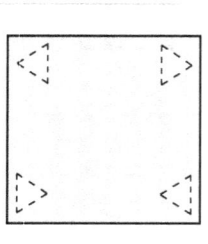

    A   B   C   D   E

7.

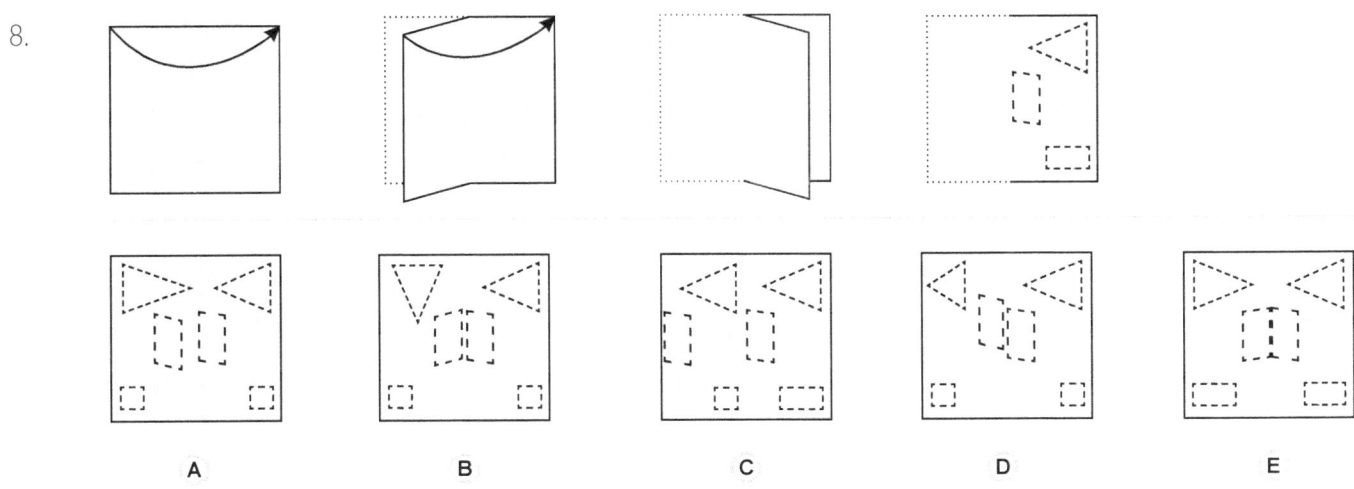

8.

9.

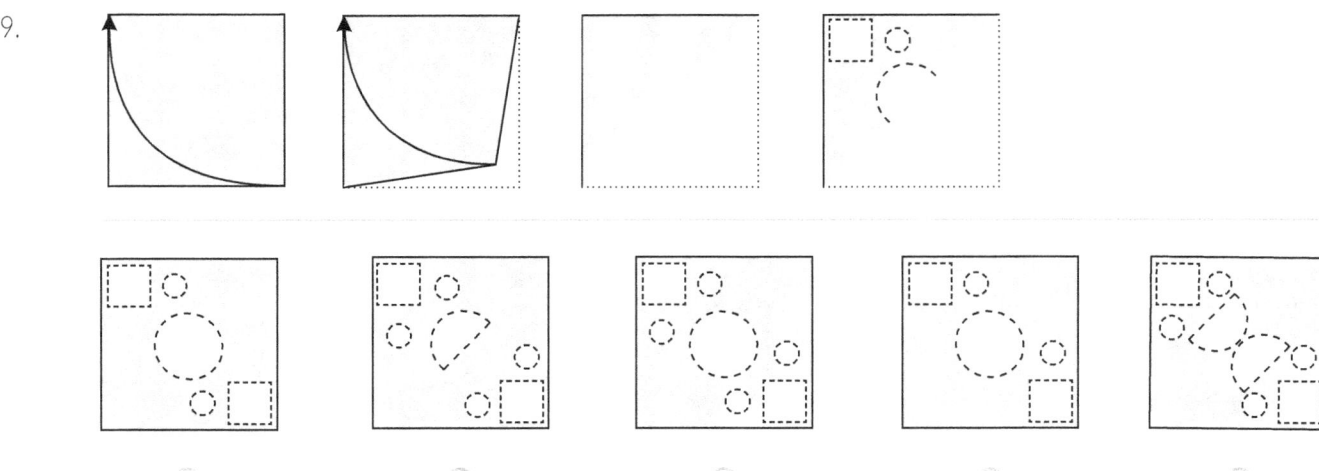

10.

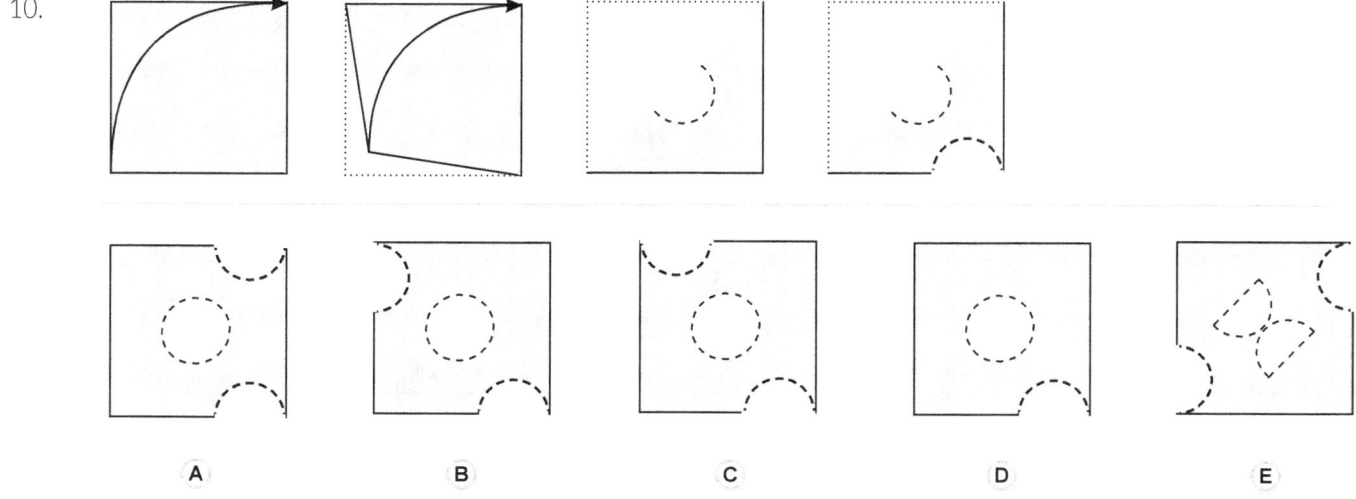

11.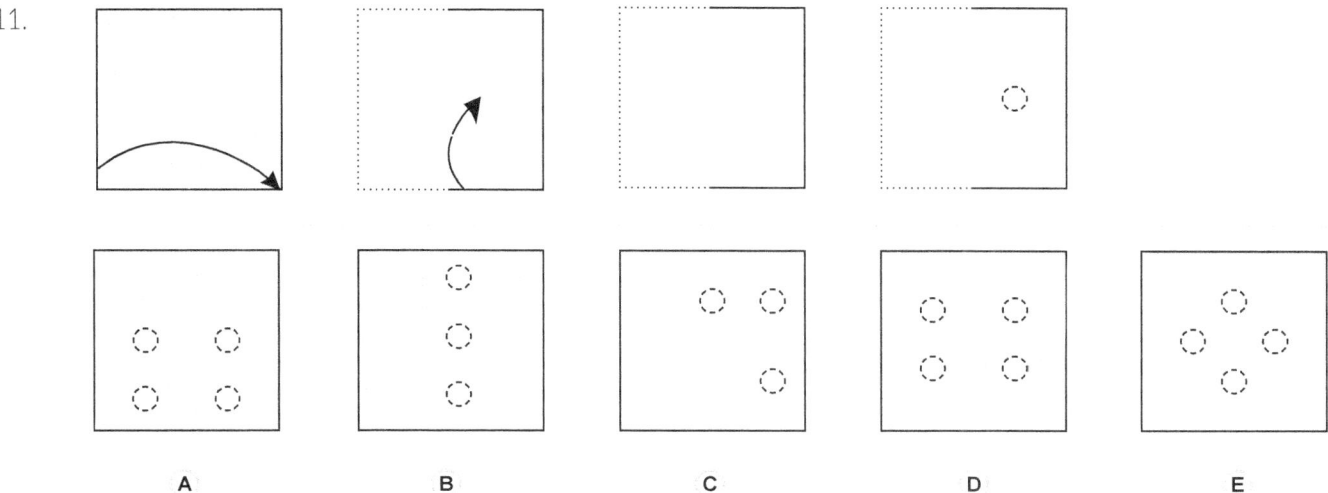

12.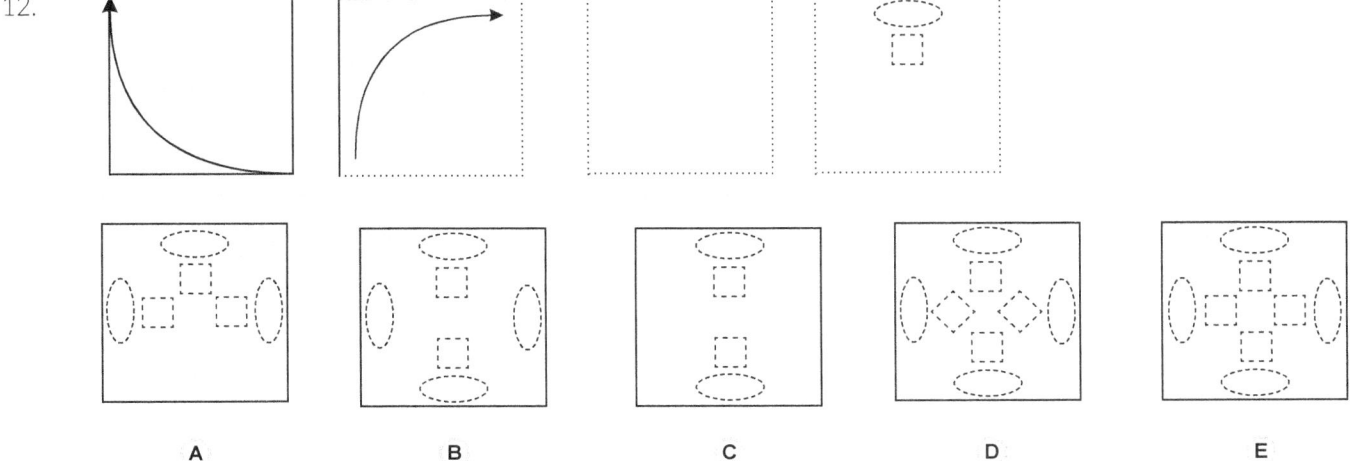

13.

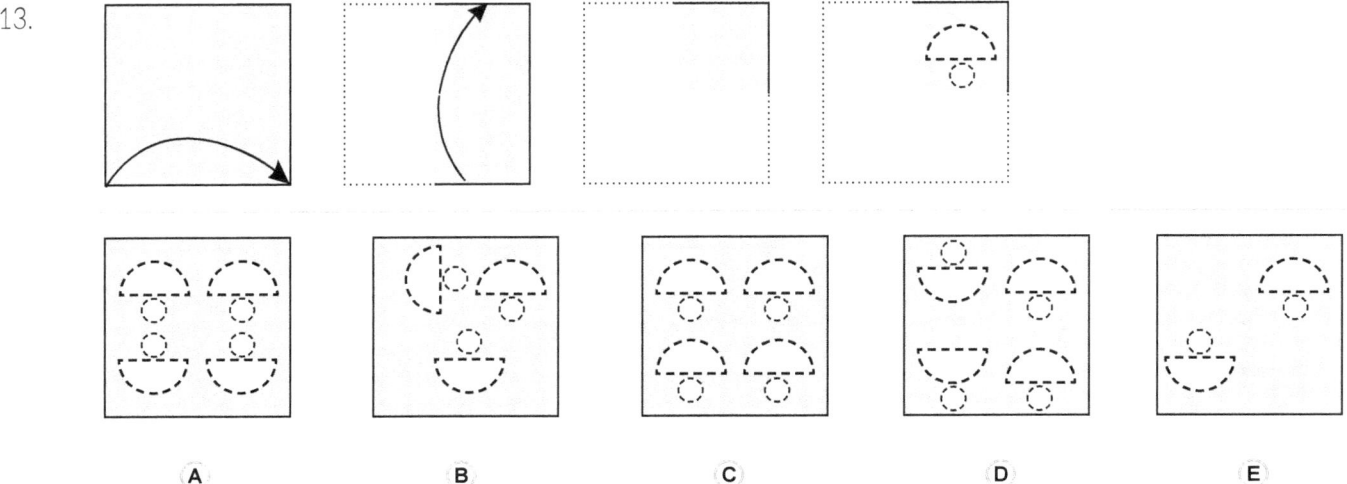

14.

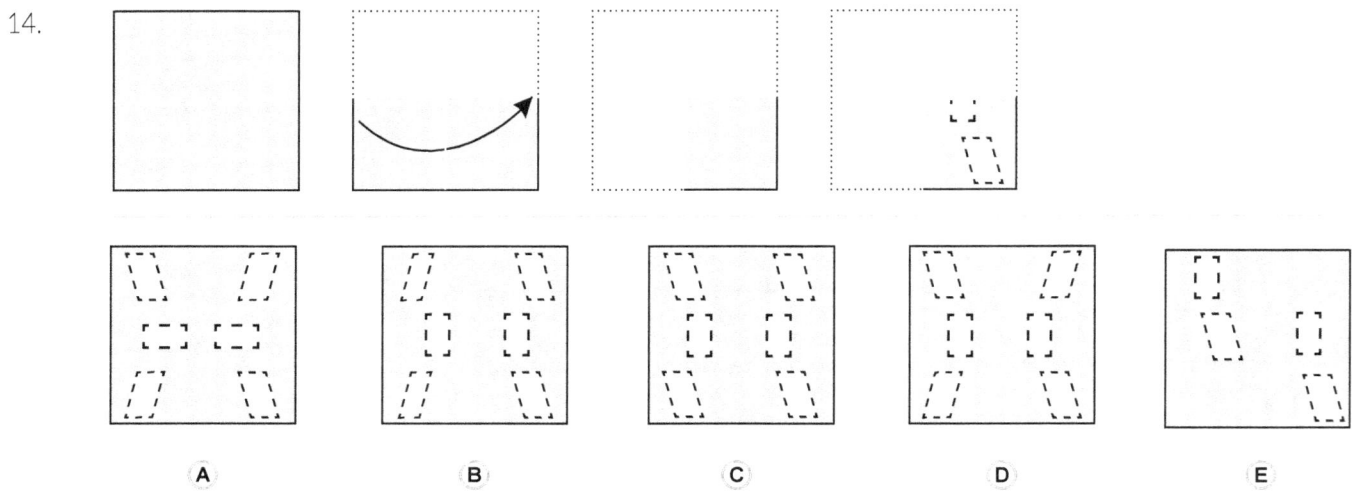

- End of Practice Test 3 -

COGAT® PRACTICE TEST ANSWER KEYS

ANSWER KEY FOR PRACTICE TEST 1 (WORKBOOK FORMAT)

Figure Analogies, Practice Test 1

-1. A. There are 3 shapes that alternate in color: gray, white, gray.

-2. B. Gray turns white, and white turns gray.

-3. C. The top and middle shapes switch position.

-4. D. The shape group rotates 90 degrees clockwise.

-5. B. The shape group rotates 90 degrees clockwise, and the top 2 shapes turn gray.

-6. C. The 2 smaller shapes align horizontally. The colors/designs of the larger outer shape and the 2 smaller shapes switch (dots/white on top and white/gray on bottom).

-7. B. A gray square becomes a white circle and vice versa. The bottom shape changes color (white to gray on top & gray to white on bottom).

-8. A. The larger outer shape becomes the smallest inner shape. The smallest inner shape becomes the larger outer shape.

-9. E. In the divided square, the objects in the top left and the bottom right switch positions (the triangle & diamond on top and the star & hexagon on bottom).

-10. C. The shape gets flatter and its colors switch.

-11. D. The gray larger shape disappears. The white shape turns gray and rotates 180 degrees.

-12. C. The colors of the shapes switch. The shape group rotates 180 degrees.

-13. A. In the divided square, the objects in the top left and the bottom right switch positions (the oval & crescent on top and the cross & diamond on bottom). Also, the objects in the upper right and lower left switch positions (the hexagon & star on top and the octagon & half circle on bottom).

-14. E. A gray heart becomes a lined triangle and vice versa. The bottom shape changes its design (lined to gray on top & gray to lined on bottom).

-15. E. An arrow point is removed.

-16. B. The octagons switch color from dark gray to filled with lines and from filled with lines to dark gray. The shape in the lower left corner changes from square filled with lines to a dark gray circle on top. On the bottom, it changes from a dark gray square to a circle filled with lines.

-17. B. In the shape groups, gray turns to white and vertical lines turn to gray.

-18. D. The shape group "flips" to become a mirror image. On the bottom, the flip occurs, but it is not noticeable because of the design of the white squares and dotted squares.

-19. A. The shape groups rotate 90 degrees clockwise and 1 more black line with a circle on the end is added to the group.

Figure Classification, Practice Test 1

-1. B. The shapes are gray.
-2. C. The shapes are divided in half.
-3. D. The shapes have one-fourth that's gray.
-4. E. Three ovals are gray, and two are white.
-5. B. The shapes have 8 sides.
-6. C. There are 3 shapes in the group.
-7. D. In each group, there are 2 shapes that are the same. These 2 shapes are next to each other.
-8. E. There's a small oval in the middle of the shape group.
-9. B. The arrow group has 4 points.
-10. B. In each shape group, there's 1 (and only 1) gray square.
-11. A. The black line is next to the base of the arrow point.
-12. E. There are 2 (and only 2) small shapes: a white heart and a black cross.
-13. D. The large shape and the small shapes are different colors.
-14. A. There are 2 black bars and 1 gray bar.
-15. D. The group of 3 shapes consists of: 1 large shape and 2 small versions of that same shape.
-16. D. Straight arrows with 1 arrow point.
-17. E. The triangles point the same way.
-18. C. The shapes have 4 sides.
-19. B. Two crescents are gray. Two are filled with lines.
-20. B. There are 2 (and only 2) small shapes: a half-circle and an octagon.

Paper Folding, Practice Test 1

1. B
2. C
3. B
4. D
5. B
6. D
7. A
8. A
9. C
10. D
11. C
12. B
13. C
14. A
15. D

ANSWER KEY FOR PRACTICE TEST 2

Figure Analogies, Practice Test 2

-1. C. The shapes align vertically. The smaller and larger shapes switch positions, sizes, and colors.

-2. D. The shape rotates 90 degrees counterclockwise.

-3. D. The thin gray shape moves behind the larger dark gray shape.

-4. A. A shape with one more side appears. (On top, a trapezoid with 4 sides becomes a pentagon with 5 sides. On the bottom, a hexagon with 6 sides becomes a heptagon with 7 sides.)

-5. D. On top, the wavy lines come together and rotate 90 degrees. On the bottom, the opposite happens – the wavy lines move apart – and rotate 90 degrees.

-6. C. The shape colors change like this: light gray becomes white, dark gray becomes light gray, and white becomes dark gray.

-7. C. The number of arrow points equals the number of sides the shape in the second box has.

-8. B. The shapes that remain are those that are light gray in the first box. They turn dark gray.

-9. A. In the 2 groups of triangles (the top group and the bottom group), 1 triangle is added on top and 1 triangle is taken away on the bottom.

-10. B. Two top shapes in the right column are removed.

-11. D. The shape group rotates 90 degrees clockwise. (In the answer choices, notice how the heart rotates.)

-12. A. The shapes change like this: Shape 1 becomes Shape 3. Shape 2 becomes Shape 4 and "flips." Shape 3 becomes Shape 2. Shape 4 becomes Shape 1 and "flips."

-13. C. The smaller shapes move inside the square and position near where they were. They also stay the same size (note how some of the choices have larger squares).

-14. A. In the divided square, the objects in the top left and the bottom right switch positions. Also, the objects in the upper right and lower left switch positions.

-15. E. One-quarter of the circle is removed. (So, after the last quarter is removed, nothing remains.)

-16. E. The group of circles "flips" to become a mirror-image, and one more circle is added.

-17. A. The logic is "1 more is added." On the top, a shape with one more side appears (a triangle with 3 sides becomes a trapezoid with 4 sides). On the bottom, one more line is added.

-18. B. The number of shapes is reduced by half and the "Xs" are removed.

-19. C. The inner white lines change from crossing similar to an "x" shape to crossing similar to a "t" shape. On the bottom, the opposite happens: they first cross similar to a "t," then cross similar to an "x."

-20. B. The smaller shape moves to the opposite corner of the larger gray shape. The inner diagonal lines go the opposite direction.

Figure Classification, Practice Test 2

-1. C. The shapes have angled corners. (Choice A, B, and E are circles/ovals and have no corners. Choice D has rounded corners.)

-2. A. There are 4 shapes in the group.

-3. D. The diamond in the shape group is in the middle of the white square.

-4. D. There are 2 (and only 2) black stars. They are either next to each other or adjacent to each other.

-5. B. The triangles form 3-in-a-row either horizontally, vertically, or diagonally.

-6. E. As the shape group rotates, the gray shape remains at the same spot on the crescent.

-7. A. The gray shape and black shape are different types of shapes.

-8. D. The shapes have 6 sides.

-9. A. The group of squares has: 1 filled with lines, 2 that are white and empty, and 1 that has a small black shape in the center.

-10. E. The left and right sections of the circle have the same shape. The top and bottom sections of the circle have the same shape.

-11. D. Inside the white square are 3 shapes that alternate in color: gray, white, gray.

-12. C. In the group of 3 shapes, 2 are the same and 1 is different. The two shapes that are the same are next to each other.

-13. B. The diagonal lines go from lower left to upper right.

-14. A. Three triangles point down, and one points up.

-15. D. The 2 smaller shapes are: 1 triangle and 1 rectangle.

-16. C. The white bar is next to where the lines of the M (or the lines of the W) come together.

-17. A. There are 3 intersecting lines inside the shape.

-18. E. There is 1 (and only 1) gray circle in the group of 3 shapes.

-19. D. Each of the 3 shapes has 1 of these designs inside: dots, diagonal lines, or gray.

-20. D. The outer shape has 1 more side than the inner shape.

Paper Folding, Practice Test 2

1. A	2. D	3. B	4. E	5. B
6. E	7. C	8. D	9. B	10. B
11. C	12. A	13. B	14. E	

ANSWER KEY FOR PRACTICE TEST 3

Figure Analogies, Practice Test 3

-1. E. A heart is added on top of the larger shape.

-2. B. The bottom shape gets larger and becomes the outer shape. The top shape becomes the middle shape and gets larger. The heart moves inside the middle shape, then rotates 90 degrees clockwise.

-3. E. The white shapes turn gray and align horizontally, with the smallest shapes on the right and the largest shapes on the left.

-4. C. The colors switch.

-5. E. The number of points equals the number of shape sides.

-6. B. In the group of 3 shapes (rectangles or ovals), the bottom shape moves to the top of the shape group. Or, you could also say that the designs of the shapes change like this: gray becomes black, dotted becomes gray, and black becomes dotted.

-7. A. The colors of the small shape and large shape switch. The large shape and small shape change to become shapes with one more side.

-8. B. The larger gray shape disappears. The remaining white shape rotates 90 degrees clockwise and turns gray.

-9. E. The larger gray shape disappears. The remaining gray shape gets bigger.

-10. D. A group of vertically-aligned small black circles appears. The number of black circles equals the number of gray shapes in the set.

-11. D. The design/color of the small and large shapes switch.

-12. C. One more gray oval is added to the group.

-13. B. The large shape becomes the color of the small shape. The small shape disappears.

-14. A. The inner shape of the shape group gets larger and wider. The outer shape of the shape group gets smaller and turns gray.

-15. B. The outer shape of the shape group gets smaller and moves to the center of the other shape.

-16. C. The figures rotate 180 degrees.

-17. A. In the shape groups (2 parallelograms on top; a parallelogram and an oval on bottom), the left shape disappears (parallelograms). The remaining shape turns black.

-18. C. The inner and outer shapes switch colors. The outer shape then becomes a shape with one more side.

-19. E. The larger gray shape becomes 2 smaller versions of this shape. In this new group of 2, however, one of the shapes is much smaller than the other. The smaller of the 2 is on top. The center white shape gets bigger. The 2 shapes are inside the larger white shape.

-20. C. The colors switch.

Figure Classification, Practice Test 3

-1. E. The shapes are divided in half.
-2. B. The bottom shape is the same as the top shape, but it has rotated 90 degrees counter-clock-wise.
-3. A. The small circle and small triangle are in opposite sections of the divided circle.
-4. E. The shapes are divided into a white section and a gray section. In the white section is a smaller version of the large shape, and it is white.
-5. D. The diagonal lines inside the shapes go from upper left to lower right.
-6. E. The gray line is just above the 2 black circles (the part of the shape that forms the base of the letter "W").
-7. C. One-fourth of the shape is filled with dots.
-8. E. Each shape group has 1 arrow, 1 hexagon, and 1 trapezoid. There is 1 (and only 1) shape of each design: wavy lines, dotted lines, and gray.
-9. B. The small shapes inside the grid are: 1 octagon and 1 parallelogram that must be next to each other and 1 star that is not next to either of the other shapes.
-10. D. The circles are divided into equal parts.
-11. A. In the group of 4 triangles, 3 point left and 1 points right.
-12. D. The shape group has the same kind of small shape in the middle.
-13. A. The 3 shapes are 3-D shapes. There is one of each color: gray, white, black. Also, there is one of each type: cube, pyramid, rectangular prism.
-14. B. The same arrow rotates clockwise/counterclockwise. (Note that in the other choices, compared to the arrows in the top row, the white/gray is on the wrong side.)
-15. B. The shapes are cut in half. The dividing white line goes diagonally from the upper left to lower right.
-16. E. There are 3 letters in the group: B, V, T. There is 1 of each color/design: gray, black, and lined.
-17. C. Each shape group has a triangle and a small heart. They must be different colors.
-18. D. Inside the circle/oval are 2 triangles that are the same color.
-19. C. There are 3 shapes in the group.
-20. C. The shapes have rounded lines and corners (compared to choices A, B, D, and E, which all have angled corners and all straight lines).

Paper Folding, Practice Test 3

1. C
2. E
3. A
4. B

5. C
6. D
7. A
8. E
9. D
10. B
11. A
12. E
13. A
14. D

Need more practice?

• Get **300+ <u>new</u> questions** per book!

• Check out more **Savant Test Prep**™ books on Amazon®.

www.ingramcontent.com/pod-product-compliance
Lightning Source LLC
Chambersburg PA
CBHW081722120626
46550CB00010B/3215